# When Teachers Reflect

*Journeys toward Effective, Inclusive Practice*

Elizabeth A. Tertell, Susan M. Klein,
and Janet L. Jewett, Editors

*A 1998 NAEYC Comprehensive Membership Benefit*

NATIONAL ASSOCIATION FOR THE EDUCATION OF YOUNG CHILDREN
WASHINGTON, D.C.

*Photo credits:* Hildegard Adler 7; Judy Burr 12; Renaud Thomas 18, 153; Eva Anthony 21; Robert Hill 29; Subjects & Predicates 42, 73; Steve Herzog 53; Michael Siluk 49, 61; April S. Haase 77; Marilyn Nolt 86, 122; Francis Wardle 91; Richard Wallace 94; Nancy P. Alexander 103, 114; Jeanette Stone 110; Susan M. Klein 126, 136; Elisabeth Nichols 133; BmPorter/Don Franklin 145; Cris M. Kelly 148; Jean Berlfein 156; Blakely Fetridge Bundy 166; Paula Jorde Bloom 172; T. Dingman 181.

**National Association for the Education of Young Children**
**1509 16th Street, NW**
**Washington, DC 20036-1426**
**800-424-2460 or 202-232-8777**
**Website: http://www.naeyc.org**

Through its publications program the National Association for the Education of Young Children (NAEYC) attempts to provide a forum for discussion of major issues and ideas in the early childhood field, with the hope of provoking thought and promoting professional growth. The views expressed or implied are not necessarily those of the Association. NAEYC thanks the editors and contributors who donated much time and effort to develop this book as a contribution to the profession.

Library of Congress Catalog Number: 98-84152

ISBN: 0-935989-85-4

NAEYC #236

Editor: Carol Copple; Design and production: Jack Zibulsky; Cover design: Sandi Collins.

**Printed in the United States of America**

**W**e dedicate this book to our families—

Tertell • Bailey

Klein • Agranoff • Shuster • Sirull

Jewett • Nitti

# About the Editors

**Elizabeth A. Tertell,** M. Ed., C.A.S., is an early childhood consultant in the metropolitan Chicago area. She has been a child care teacher, a center and program director, and an adult educator working with teachers, directors, and families. For two years she served as coordinator of Indiana's Best Practices in Integration—Outreach project, a training model in which this book's mentors and contributors participated.

**Susan M. Klein**, Ph. D., is a professor of special education at Indiana University in Bloomington, where she directs the graduate teacher education program and the doctoral specialization in early childhood special education. She also serves as a member of the state leadership team directing a statewide system of professional development in early childhood special education.

**Janet L. Jewett,** Ph. D., has worked as a child care teacher, a teacher trainer, an early childhood specialist at a regional laboratory, and an inclusion facilitator for a statewide training and technical assistance project. Presently she teaches courses in early childhood and special education and supervises the field work of students at Washington State University in Vancouver.

# ... and Mentors

**Darla Cohen,** M.S., is a parent of three children with special needs. Currently she is a trainer for Indiana's early intervention and early childhood special education professional development system through Indiana University.

**Tamyra Freeman,** M.A., has worked with a number of community organizations in facilitating collaboration. Currently she is a training consultant for several Indiana organizations, including Greenleaf Center for Servant-Leadership and the Indiana Parent Information Network.

**Darcee Hume-Thoren,** M.S., formerly a kindergarten teacher, is a training consultant in early childhood for colleges and universities in Indiana.

# Contents

# Acknowledgments

To the teachers who wrote with such candor and thoughtfulness. Their stories, written in 1995, reflect where they were at that point in time, not where they are today. Their willingness to share with readers their early journeys, complete with self-doubts and evolving practice, is what makes this book possible.

To our colleagues Darla Cohen, Tamyra Freeman, Darcee Hume-Thoren, and Susan Miner for their various roles throughout the course of the project and beyond.

To Carol Copple and Millie Riley at NAEYC for their expertise in editorial matters and their never-ending enthusiasm for this book.

To DeAnna Stephens, Barb Zivat, and Aileen Kocanda for their technical support.

To Susan McBride, Sharon Rosenkoetter, and Eva Thorpe who early on encouraged us to gather and share teachers' stories as part of our outreach project evaluation.

To Susan Kontos whose interest and commitment to the project never wavered.

To Cathy Gruber, Ellie Nolan, and Pam Leffers for sharing their expertise in early childhood and adult education.

To Kate Kressley for her energy and determination in assisting with the original proposal development and submission.

There are many who have helped us on our journeys. We thank the multitude of colleagues, mentors, and friends for their influences in our lives.

# Preface

This is a book about being committed to meeting the individual needs of all children. It's about being inclusive, letting all children know that "You have the right to be here, not hidden in the back room; we want to know you and see your strengths and wholeness." It's about the kind of educational settings we want for all children—engaging and developmentally appropriate communities of learners. Every one of us is involved in the process of change. In this volume each teacher reflects on her or his journey toward becoming a better teacher. They share portions of their individual journeys in seeking to be excellent and inclusive teachers of young children—like works in progress. They start each of their journeys in a different place, go their own direction, and travel at their own pace.

No journey is yet complete. Herein lies the essence—a state of not being done—that we support and share with you. Individual and collective perspectives give insight. Each writer chose to engage in the process of reflecting on and documenting her or his individual growth. They have continued to grow and change since they shared their stories in this book. Each one's efforts encourage us all in using reflective and collaborative processes to begin or continue on our own journeys.

The three of us—Susan Klein, Liz Tertell, and Jan Jewett—found each other through our passionate commitment to being inclusive and promoting adults' change. We brought different perspectives and expertise to our collaboration. Our varied experiences and common vision made for a productive combination and included a shared valuing of emergent curriculum, respect for adults and children, inclusion, the power of process, opportunities to reflect and collaborate, and the co-construction of knowledge.

This opportunity to collaborate began with Susan and her work at Indiana University on the Best Practices in Integration—Outreach project, which focused on the changing skills needed by early childhood special educators to teach young learners with special needs. As the focus shifted to exploring how to support adults in their development and improved practice with respect to inclusion, she connected with Liz. Liz contributed her perspectives on the process of assisting adults to change their professional practices and her experiences in early childhood education and adult training and support for change. Liz introduced Susan to her colleague Jan Jewett, an early childhood educator and adult training specialist.

Through our new connection the three of us had many conversations about the process of adult change in issues relating to inclusion and went on to discuss these issues with other colleagues. Liz and Susan began a process of transforming the original training delivery system (a series of training modules developed by Susan with Susan Kontos) into an emergent-curriculum model. In our dialogue we examined the processes of collaboration and reflection to explore how these contribute to the process of adults' change. Key features of our redesigned training system were (1) identifying common needs and concerns of participants; (2) redefining a training session's content based on participant concerns; (3) combining disciplines to enable special educators and early childhood educators to meet collaboratively in training sessions; (4) increasing participants' ownership and active participation; (5) promoting and using collaborative processes throughout the training; and (6) focusing on the reflective process in learning and its contributions to change.

We discovered that hearing others talk about their challenges in creating inclusive settings is a powerful impetus to change. Such dialogues and reflections give teachers encouragement to think about their practice. Making this book a collective project is our way of continuing to engage in the adult learning process. As a collective process it also has provided a means for evaluating the work the project set out to accomplish.

Themes addressed in Chapters 1 through 7 were identified by the communities that participated in the outreach training project. The topics covered in these chapters are major themes in early childhood inclusion efforts: play, guidance, individualizing, including everyone, emergent curriculum, working with families, and collaboration. Each chapter includes the reflections of several teachers on their own journeys, particularly with respect to one topic—be it guidance, individualizing, or one of the other themes. Serving as mentors were the editors and three adult trainers—Darla Cohen, Tamyra Freeman, and Darcee Hume-Thoren—each with an expertise related to a specific topic.

The teachers who agreed to write their reflections were participants in the project's outreach training, either directly or indirectly. Some applied this work in their graduate studies. All of them thought through and wrote their own stories; their mentors acted as collaborators, provocateurs, and supporters. In the process the mentors struggled with their own issues, concerns, and problems.

As you read what the teachers have written from their experiences, you will have your own responses. Following each teacher's contribution is a reflection by the mentor. Sometimes these responses will echo your own. In other instances they may bring up points you haven't noticed, or you may have an entirely different response or observation. Each section closes with questions or activities that may be useful as you consider the teacher's story and the issues that arise related to the chapter's topic. We have included possibilities that reflect various styles of thinking and reflecting and expect that each individual will resonate with certain activities more than with others. Activities can be used individually, in groups, or in training sessions.

The Prologue provides a frame for discussing issues related to change and describes the context within which the teachers' stories emerged. Each chapter can be read and used on its own. It is our hope that this book supports you the reader as you make your own journey toward effective, inclusive practice.

—*The Editors*

# Prologue

*Susan M. Klein, Elizabeth A. Tertell,*
*and Janet L. Jewett*

## Susan Klein/Inclusion through Collaboration

When I first chose to pursue a master's in special education, I had not anticipated the passion for the field that would emerge. As a teenager I had worked at a camp for children with special needs and later taught preschool children with autism. The more I was immersed in the field, the more my interest and commitment grew.

I watched with satisfaction and joy as the predecessor of the Individuals with Disabilities Education Act, Public Law 94-142, was passed in 1975 and later amended (IDEA Amendments 1991), leading to the emergence of a discipline identified as early childhood special education. For several years then I helped design and implement early intervention programs and preschool programs for very young children at risk or with special needs and support networks for their families. All the while I encouraged adults to expand their professional expertise in working with these children and families. Enthusiastically I joined the groundswell of interest and advocacy for community integration of young children with special needs and devoted my energies to implementing this approach.

As public and professional opinion shifted toward integration, now called *inclusion* or *supported education,* it became less clear who should be the teacher for young children with special needs. Should it be an early childhood special education teacher or an early childhood teacher who would have children with special needs integrated within the regular preschool setting? In Indiana I worked to foster the professional role of "teacher of young children with special needs" and encourage practitioners to seek professional development opportunities and inservice training.

## Fostering inclusion through professional development and community involvement

In collaboration with Susan Kontos, a colleague in the Department of Child Development and Family Studies at Purdue University, I helped to develop a model project with a cross-disciplinary, inclusive approach to serving preschool children with special needs in integrated, community-based settings. The intent was to broaden the knowledge and skills of both early childhood intervention professionals and early childhood educators (Klein & Kontos 1993). This project continued as an outreach initiative, Best Practices in Integration–Outreach project, under my direction.

The project defined *early childhood intervention professionals* as special education administrators and teachers, physical therapists, occupational therapists, speech pathologists, health care providers, and other individuals providing specialized services or therapies to infants, toddlers, or preschoolers with developmental disabilities or at risk for a disability. The term *early childhood education professionals* includes teachers and administrators in preschools and child care programs as well as family child care home providers.

The project goal was to reach communities across the state and assist them in helping children with special needs to play and learn in settings with typically developing peers. I knew that many changes would have to take place –in professional roles, personal beliefs, and organizational systems and operations. From previous experience I knew also that meaningful inservice training needed to be based on community preparation and planning as well as appropriate training content and processes. The focus was increasing inclusive practices for *all* persons –a total community's participation in programs for education, recreation, and work. This approach would mean young children with special needs and their families having opportunities to attend community early childhood programs with the needed support services to ensure success.

## Working toward collaboration

From the project staff's collective experiences with training and varied professional backgrounds emerged key principles and beliefs about children, families, collaboration, and change that framed the development of the project's work. One fundamental principle was that changing a system involves changing the beliefs as well as the practices of both project staff and community stakeholders. The professionals' beliefs about their roles and the roles of others have a powerful effect on the process. Fostering a learning climate that enhances collaboration is challenging.

The plan was to bring individuals together in a way that would encourage *each* individual's ideas, resources, and participation. Staff sometimes perceived the project meetings as very successful and productive; at other times tension and stress prevailed. Powerful as collaboration is, achieving it is not always easy. In the process of observing people explore and struggle with their current roles, valued ideas and practices, and expectations for others, I learned greatly.

Collaborative consultation was the central concept. The project sought to teach early childhood intervention professionals about early childhood practice and educate early childhood teachers about intervention services. To build both groups' awareness of what they could achieve through collaboration and what this might look like in practice was crucial. As a project staff we envisioned early childhood intervention specialists as consultants and early childhood educators as direct-service providers, but the emphasis was seeing that the expertise of both groups was acknowledged. We would consider the project successful if all the professionals regarded the children and families involved not as *yours* or *mine* but as *ours*.

At first five instructional modules formed the core of training. A number of early childhood programs across Indiana received the modules, and although participants valued the training, they said they needed more ongoing support to make inclusion work. As a result, the project staff focused on follow-up, organizing the professionals and parents in each program into a team to enhance collaboration and give priority attention to the process of technical assistance and consultation. The collaboration itself became a very valuable part of the project, anchored continuing efforts, and enabled staff to focus the outreach project evaluation on the technical assistance and consultation process.

Liz Tertell joined the project and together with staff engaged in long deliberations about training and consultation, community uniqueness, and individual needs. With her early childhood expertise, she helped all of us at the project consider the language barriers between professions and revisit the inservice training model.

## Learning from the project

A wide variety of people and communities participated in the outreach project. Our experiences with them have taught us a great deal about the design and evaluation of training. Now the project's training is community-driven and more personalized. With respect to training, the experience confronted me with challenges in these areas: (1) assuming different roles and other aspects of the change process, (2) adult training approaches and moving beyond the "expert" model, and (3) the process of reflection and collaboration in the teaching and learning process.

Very often trainers assume that individuals being trained to take on new roles are eager, ready, and able to make such transitions. Many teachers in this project found role shifting—like relocation—to be painful, stressful, and difficult; many resisted. Individuals involved in role change need opportunities to explore the effects of change on their organization and program and on their individual roles. From the project's beginning it was clear that training and support were needed in creating collaborative consultation, but how much and in what ways the change process would influence the roles and organizational functioning of the trainees' work settings was not foreseen.

I gained personally, learning a great deal about adult training, specifically technical assistance and the concept of consultation. In providing technical assistance, project staff encouraged professionals to engage in collaborative problem solving. But many trainees found it difficult seeing *each* participant in the training process as having expertise. They had prior perceptions of themselves and others in terms of skills and knowledge, and these perceptions influenced their own behavior and expectations. Some people took on the expert role; other individuals continually deferred. Grappling with this issue was an important challenge.

Teacher education students have long kept journals in my graduate courses —speaking in their own voices to critically examine their own teaching practices. But more recently I discovered the great value of their sharing and discussing their journals and reflections with each other and then adding to their own journals further reflection on this collaborative and interactive process.

Perceiving all the adults as collaborative researchers strengthened the training project. Rebecca New's description of teachers as collaborators encouraged and inspired this approach, as did the input of colleagues involved in similar inservice training efforts (Mallory & New 1994). Keeping a journal became the means of telling the outreach project's story (Klein, Tertell, & Jewett 1995). All project participants documented their own practices and the collaborative nature of their interactions with each other.

Throughout this project I have learned to listen to early childhood educators as they talk about their challenges. I have reexamined my ideas about what works best for children with special needs and cast aside my script. I have done a lot of thinking about the role of teacher as learner, my own role as teacher-learner, and the relationship between teachers' needs and how they teach. I expect to continue this process throughout my career.

# Liz Tertell/Reflections on Adult Learning

As a child care teacher and a Head Start and child care director, I had worked with children with special needs. But I hardly considered myself an expert, certainly not sufficiently expert to develop training on inclusive classrooms. After becoming coordinator for the Best Practices in Integration —Outreach project, with some hesitation, I gradually began to look at inclusive classrooms in a new way. Thinking about the inclusive classroom as I would any classroom —not as entirely different —enabled me to focus on what *all* teachers need to know and think about in their own settings.

## The value of belonging

This process toward inclusion has encouraged me to think more about classrooms, teaching, families, and young children. One of my strongest concerns has been the social and emotional development of young children and adults, especially the sense of belonging and being valued by the group. As a teacher, then a director, and now a trainer, I have sought to value both the uniqueness of the individual and the diversity of those in the group, while at the same time drawing everyone together as a community. The task is not easy, but valuing it has caused me to rethink my planning, approach, and style.

As I look at belonging, I see two sides. There is the cognitive side, which involves learning about the inclusive, antibias approach and thinking about what happens in programs. And there is the affective side—our emotional reactions to belonging and not belonging, in our own lives and the lives of others. Like most people, I have memories, beginning in childhood, of not belonging. I can cry with a child who doesn't feel included, be angry when parents are judged, and feel ashamed and guilty when I have not valued what everyone has to offer. Both sides matter, and both have shaped the project's approach and the path we have each taken.

## Entering foreign territory

As the new project coordinator, I visited inclusive programs; talked to staff, children, and parents; and listened to the "real" inclusion experts. The first few months I often felt like a foreigner learning a new language and finding my way around. I carried a notebook with me, writing down my questions and listing all the words or references I didn't understand in this new context. Sometimes the words weren't words at all, but acronyms such as LRE (least restrictive environment) or FAPE (free and appropriate public education). Everyone talked about IEPs (individual education plans) and IFSPs (individual family service plans). I jotted down what I didn't comprehend and later asked staff members to translate for me into language I could understand.

Before long I realized it wasn't such a new land after all. Although some language sounded different, I was hearing issues I had heard often in the early childhood world: listening to and involving parents; issues concerning discipline, individualization, and planning and implementing curriculum in day-to-day instruction. All teachers struggle with these questions of "How do we work with others when we disagree with their philosophy?" and "How do we create classrooms that are unbiased?"

The world of special education and inclusion was new to me, but understanding early childhood education and young children and families let me cross the bridge into this territory. I saw that I had always worked in settings where inclusion existed. Perhaps we didn't *plan* the inclusion, but we did what made sense for children and families. Now I appreciate the need we all have to *think* about inclusion, reflect on our practices, and be intentional about what we are doing and the classrooms we are creating.

I recognize that the two worlds of early childhood and special education are not so different after all. Although one needs special information and knowledge to create high-quality inclusive settings, the first step is a commitment to inclusion and meeting the individual needs of children and families.

## Co-constructing collaborative training and support

As my view of inclusive classrooms changed, so did the training in the project. To develop the training, I thought about my own experiences as well as the issues and experiences of the practitioners who were going to be working in more inclusive settings. I began by acknowledging that I didn't have the inclusion answer. There wasn't a recipe everyone could follow to make classrooms inclusive, rather it was good practices —developmentally appropriate practices —and culturally sensitive curricula that made inclusive classrooms. I also believed that if teachers were reflective —thinking about their values, beliefs, and practices —inclusiveness would flourish in their classrooms. I based my planning on these very simple beliefs: reflective practitioners use good practices and good practices are beneficial for all children.

Next, I thought about the importance of adult learners participating in shaping their own learning. Instead of planning in advance what information to present, I decided to find out what teachers wanted to learn and thought they needed to know. For example, some were eager to learn more about working with families; others wanted a more in-depth understanding of play; and virtually everyone found discipline a continuing challenge.

Such issues voiced by participants shaped how I went about developing community-based training. I did not develop workshops on specific disabilities or diagnoses such as autism, Down syndrome, or attention deficit hyperactivity disorder. After all, children with any one of these disabilities are by no means identical, and I didn't want to pigeonhole them in teachers' minds. In addition, the teachers being trained from the special education field already had this knowledge and expertise, and I was building collaborations, not coming in and giving the one answer.

Believing that parents know their child best and often know more than teachers do about the child's needs, I wanted to encourage teachers to listen to what family members want for their child. Some families, for instance, might be more concerned about social development than about academic gains. To collaborate with parents requires respecting their concerns.

Technical assistance was the best avenue for addressing individual issues such as creating a plan for a child with autism or responding to other child-specific needs. More global issues, such as supporting parents and collaborating with other professionals, were addressed directly in the training.

We also recognized the importance of actually developing collaborative relationships between special education and early childhood educators, not just talking about it. By sharing our expertise, we all learned more.

## Designing training

I began the training design by exploring the interest of communities in getting involved in the Best Practices project. I spoke to principals, child care and preschool directors, special education directors, Head Start staff, social workers, and community leaders. Based on interest, we invited the participation of teachers and teacher assistants plus support staff, including speech and hearing therapists, and directors and supervisors. Through interviews, observations, and surveys of participants, we assessed the concerns and used this information to develop the training topics. Each community decided the best times and dates to meet. The sessions were facilitated by myself, other project staff, or outside consultants.

All of the training incorporated an emphasis on reflection. Each participant kept a journal focused on an issue he or she wanted to focus on. Chosen issues were usually, but not always, ones that had been discussed at a workshop. Participants also made a choice to work with a mentor, by themselves, or in a group. They decided the style of their own journals. Some created a reflection using pictures and images; others put their reflections into words; still others documented their journeys on audio- or videotape. The goal was to further thinking and reflect on one's journey, not to bring everyone on the same journey.

There were many questions, anxieties, and concerns. It is difficult for any one of us to document the occasions that, in retrospect, make us uncomfortable and less than proud. It can be distressing too to think about people reading, possibly criticizing, or worse yet not understanding! But the stories we tell about our own growth and development help others learn and grow.

## Lessons learned

Working with a group of adults, I have a tendency to get excited about ideas we're discussing. In the past I often lost sight of how much time, energy, and emotion participants had invested in their own teaching. I might say, "Isn't this great?" and "Doesn't this give us something to think about?" but the teachers were feeling, "I thought I was doing my best in my classroom." In my eagerness to offer teachers ideas, I neglected to show adequate respect for the thinking and doing many had been engaged in long before entering this training. Some ambivalence, questioning, and discomfort were to be expected, but when people feel threatened they become resistant. Teachers are more open to change when they receive trust, respect, and the time and safety to make mistakes and grow.

Bill Ayers, an early childhood professor at the University of Illinois–Chicago, speaks about viewing children as whole persons instead of focusing on limitations, seeing individuals as three-dimensional instead of flat or one-sided. Hearing his talk during this project struck a deep chord in me. I realized that I viewed teachers as flat, wanting to "fill" teachers, to fix the places where they were not complete —what they didn't know and what I thought they should know. I was applying a deficit model to adult training.

It is difficult to reflect on how I used to approach training. I wanted to help create classrooms in which children become researchers and active participants, but I didn't always show teachers that same trust. Having learned this, I am now engaging teachers in a process of co-constructing knowledge —facilitating, provoking, and supporting. I encourage small changes, for I know they lead to continued learning and development. I am able to step back and give the time for processing knowledge instead of rushing it. I understand that all adults are at different places in their learning continuum and need different things from me and from the training sessions. I look for ways to build on strengths, abilities, and learning styles to see the wholeness of teaching styles and approaches. In wanting to provide a rich, safe environment for teachers' growth, I am changing my own role in the process.

## Jan Jewett/Change and the Reflection Process

When I taught nineteen 3- to 5-year-olds in child care, my co-teacher and I often put out table activities that were somewhat self-maintaining and captured the interests of this mixed-age group. Then we could be available to children instead of always managing activities or materials.

A favorite table activity involved eyedroppers, food colors, and plastic egg cartons or ice cube trays with all compartments filled with water. The idea was to engage children in the science of color mixing. The children seemed quite interested in this activity and came often to the table to explore it.

One day as I rinsed used containers, I noticed 5-year-old Danny still experimenting with the materials. He had worked intently with a tray and eyedropper for quite a while. I congratulated myself on the excellent job we had done in offering a color-mixing activity so perfectly matched to Danny's interest. Suddenly, he exclaimed excitedly, "I did it! I finally did it!" "What did you do, Danny?" I responded. "I finally got the water all the way up to the top of the dropper!" he told me with intense satisfaction and then ran off to another activity.

I was both crestfallen and amused at myself —at the difference between what I had been thinking and what had really been happening. That experience was memorable, partly because my self-congratulations received such immediate, corrective feedback.

Going on to graduate school the next year, I had many opportunities to take in new information and reflect on my professional life. Reflecting on the episode with Danny, I found it became part of a transformative experience for me. I came to understand that his experience that day had every bit as much merit as a science activity as did color mixing. For Danny it was an exploration of suction. His experience and learning were just as significant as what I had in mind when

I planned the activity. Had I been able to let go of my own intentions and teacher ego, I might have learned what Danny was pursuing and how he understood suction. Then I could have supported him in expanding and deepening his interests and understanding.

I have told this story many times in talks with professionals working with young children. We always laugh at the discrepancy between my perceptions of the activity's purpose and Danny's. It's a laugh of recognition because this is familiar territory. The talk goes on to the struggle we all face in teaching: how to balance our own ideas, goals, and assumptions with those of each unique young individual in our care. The essence of being inclusive —supporting every child's potentials for growth —is embodied in this dynamic balancing act.

What does it take to become more inclusive? After my many years in many roles and explorations, I have concluded that these are the critical components in the process of supporting children and adults as they grow: our beliefs and values, our professional skills and knowledge base, and the whole self —that system keeping the many parts in balance and enabling us to remain an integrated whole in spite of many changes.

What sustains the energy and flexibility required for engaging in such complex efforts? I have sought to understand the change process —people's willingness and ability to change and the steps or stages of change. Further, I have explored aspects of nurturing successful change.

## Change and transformation

One summer a friend with a passion for studying moths and butterflies convinced me to host three polyphemous moth caterpillars through the remainder of their life cycle. I built a container and provided a steady supply of fresh oak leaves. Within weeks the caterpillars grew larger than my thumbs, and from a room away I could hear them munching. Then the eating halted abruptly, and they began to prepare their cocoons —each caterpillar attaching itself to a branch, wrapping leaves around itself, and spinning material to bind the leaves together.

The three cocoons wintered in a container on our back porch, exposed to cold and moisture but not to predators. One survived and emerged on a spring day. Fully unfurled, its wing span was larger than my two hands.

My friend explained to me that during the cocoon stage the moth completely transforms itself. Body parts do not evolve from one form to another, but rather the entire organism restructures itself, turns into "cosmic soup," and then transforms. To me this cycle embodies intriguing aspects of the change process. Each stage is a total transformation of the individual's being and way of functioning, with its own dangers and possibilities. For example, the caterpillar eats voraciously, stores up enough energy, and protects that energy by building a safe cocoon to survive the crisis of total restructuring. As in the moth's life cycle, major change often involves qualitatively different stages of development. It requires generation and judicious use of energy; it offers powerful dangers and opportunities; and it is fundamentally and profoundly transformational.

Joseph Campbell (1973) in his *The Hero with a Thousand Faces*, discusses themes and elements such as the journey of the hero that crops up in all cultures. Exploring the common elements in various cultures' stories and symbols, he argues that they support the process of change that each individual must undergo. Real change is a heroic task. It requires individuals to give up their old ways and to make the terrifying, exhilarating leap into a new way of being or doing. Grieving and loss are inherent in change. Giving up a former way of being or doing, we face loss. We instinctively know that change can hurt, and that it can be dangerous. Yet, the process of transformation unleashes previously untapped forces and structures.

Previously contained or trapped energy, once released, may not be easy to manage. Facing change can make us fearful of pain; we may get depressed, crabby, anxious, or rigid. We may hold tight to the structures we count on to keep us safe and maintain the constancy that is familiar and comforting. Often we may ward off or reject new ideas or opportunities that threaten to change our lives. Or some of us may rush headlong into change after change, never slowing down enough to acknowledge what we're leaving behind and mourn its loss.

## When supports for change are lacking

Human cultures traditionally have provided rituals and other supports to assist individuals undergoing predictable psychic crises. Initiation into adulthood, marriage, and other developmental events were marked with rituals that gave people a frame for undergoing change. In today's society these rituals have lost much of their power and meaning, if they even still exist. We are without these psychic and social supports, yet our society generates more frequent pressures to change.

In the present age we take constant and continuous change for granted —change of residence, change in careers, change in family structure, and on and on. In our professional lives, training and technical assistance systems, distance learning, information superhighways, and a myriad of other tools help to give us the information we need to keep up with constantly changing demands. In contrast, our society offers far fewer resources or supports to enable people to examine and revitalize their beliefs and values or to deal with the upheaval that comes with change. The lack of such supports limits our ability to benefit from new information resources and technologies. We are being called upon constantly to make more changes, but we have fewer opportunities to integrate them.

Our society also dehumanizes the process of change. Training is often delivered according to the factory model: all individuals are given the same materials and experiences at the same time as if they were "like parts" moving in unison along a conveyor belt. Yet each of us approaches change differently and makes sense of new knowledge, ideas, and experiences in our own way. In my experience individuals respond best to what I call a "menu of options," deciding for them-selves how and what to seek out and use as they work through a change process.

Because our culture has discarded many of the built-in supports and traditions that helped people assimilate and integrate change, individuals must look out for themselves and find ways to meet their own needs. We each must become our own advocate, speaking out for the opportunities we need. We must take care of ourselves, manage change processes, and still maintain a reserve of sensitivity not only to our own needs but to the needs of children and families we work with.

If change is so difficult, is it okay *not* to change? Can we congratu-late ourselves on having reached the pinnacle as professionals, feeling completely satisfied with the way we are doing our job and planning to keep on doing it just this way? If the world was a static place and children were like factory parts, this might be an option. But in the real world, the needs and conditions with which children come to us change constantly, and every child is one of a kind. If we cease learn-ing about children and families and treat them in standardized ways, we fail them. And, for ourselves we cut off opportunities to grow and to expand our capabilities.

## Supporting change

Through my explorations of resources for assisting people as well as myself in undergoing change, I have found a number of helpful materials and ideas. One resource is *Taking Charge of Change* (Hord et al. 1987). The authors offer a framework for understanding the pro-cess professionals go through as they encounter educational innova-tions. They describe "stages of concern" that characterize education-related changes. First, the individual is unaware of the possibility for change. Next she or he focuses on personal and managerial concerns: What way will the change affect me? How can I manage all of this?

Finally the individual moves toward concerns about the overall impact of the change: How well is this change working? Knowing about this progression is helpful for professionals who act as change agents — that is, they are catalysts in provoking and helping others to change their professional skills and behaviors. The authors offer suggestions and strategies for how to be supportive of individuals at the various stages in their change.

Another resource, *Changing Kindergartens*, edited by Stacie Goffin and Dolores Stegelin (1992), gives case studies profiling the change process in kindergarten systems that are moving toward developmentally appropriate practice.

In understanding how to assist someone in integrating change, *Transitions: Making Sense of Life's Changes* by William Bridges is very helpful. He looks at what personal change feels like, the way a person develops and alters his or her own approach to experiencing change, and the three stages in the personal change process. In his description the first stage is an Ending, the second is The Neutral Zone, and third is New Beginnings. In other words, change begins with an ending and ends with a beginning, separated by an uncomfortable period of being in transition. The book validates both the challenges and the opportunities inherent in changing and offers techniques and strategies for optimizing a change process.

## *About reflection*

One day in a class, we were talking about how it isn't supportive of young children to make stereotypical comments about their creations, such as, "Isn't that pretty! What is it?" One student, Georgia, asked what one should say instead. We generated ideas such as describing what we saw, "I see you used a lot of red in this picture," and asking open-ended questions like, "Can you tell me about it?" The next week Georgia told us what had happened to her. She was excited to try the new approach in talking with children about their artwork and had even mentally rehearsed responses. Entering the classroom, she went over to a group of children drawing. One child eagerly showed Georgia his finished piece, and she said, "Isn't that interesting! Tell me about it! What is it?"

Georgia was frustrated and disappointed because she had been eager to use new language, and the old words popped out. Her story led to a discussion about how hard it is to change our behavior even when we have changed our attitudes, our knowledge, or our intentions. I continue both to be amazed and dismayed at the complexities involved in changing practices, and now view the reflection process as one of the linchpins of continuing professional and personal development.

The power of the reflection process in creating and improving professional skills is the focus of Donald Schön's *The Reflective Practitioner: How Professionals Think in Action* (1983). Looking at how people know what to do in the course of doing their jobs, Schön points out that professionals such as teachers develop a complex set of skills and knowledge that enables them to engage in professional practice.

In our work with young children, we encounter certain situations again and again. As we successfully respond to these situations, we gain professional stability and confidence, our reactions may become more integrated and unconscious, and we become less easily surprised. Achieving this level of automatic response to common situations is rewarding because it frees up energy and attention to focus on other things.

The danger in this easy, successful, and routine practice is that it may become more repetitive and routine, less creative and satisfying, and less responsive to the particular child or situation. Children and their families are aware of being treated in a mechanical way, just as they are conscious of our efforts to control or reduce their freedom to be themselves.

As Schön notes, professionals require much more than a discrete set of skills and knowledge because the situations in which they work are complex and always offer unique circumstances. Insightful practitioners can quickly identify challenges and problems that cannot be solved with a standard operating procedure or strategy. Schön calls such problems and challenges "messes."

In consulting with early childhood teachers, I regularly encounter this phenomenon of standardization. A teacher asked for advice, for example, about how to improve the room arrangement. Early in my career, I was so thrilled to be needed and eager to be helpful that I quickly offered specific suggestions, only to be met with a perplexed, somewhat frustrated and dubious look. I learned that any specific change, although seeming simple and clear cut to me, had complex repercussions. Moving the rarely used piano out of the room to free up space turned out to be a political act that could offend the director who used to teach in that room and was especially proud of her music curriculum. I learned that changes of this nature affected the system as a whole. I gave up trying to prescribe; rather I grew to see my role as one of trusting and supporting professionals to find their own resolution to their own complex messes.

Reflection-in-action, as Schön calls it, is a strategy that enables teachers whose usual methods are not working in a particular situation to reframe or take a more experimental approach. It provides an antidote to the pull of comfortable, familiar routines and strategies. The act of thinking back or reconsidering during a project, task, or challenging situation allows us to notice, examine, and perhaps rethink the tacit understandings that have developed around our familiar practices. In this manner teachers can make new sense out of situations and uncertainties and respond successfully to challenges. This reframing and reflection process allows more of our own re- sources —the nonverbal, creative, even the outrageous —to be applied to the unique problem at hand.

Reflection may lead to major and complex restructuring of signi- ficant components of our professional practice. We may see that for a long time we have been responding in a way that is far from optimal and experience regret over lost opportunities. We may fear the tough work ahead. Reflection is indeed a risky business, but it holds tremen- dous promise too.

When our reflections allow us to reach a new way of framing a dilemma or a new understanding, we often experience a gratifying burst of energy. We no longer feel confined to a particular way of behaving. New doors seem to open, new paths appear for exploration and discovery.

## References

Bridges, W. 1980. *Transitions: Making sense of life's changes.* Reading, MA: Addison Wesley.

Campbell, J. 1973. *The hero with a thousand faces.* Princeton, NJ: Princeton University Press.

Goffin, S., & D. Stegelin. 1992. *Changing kindergartens: Four success stories.* Washing- ton, DC: NAEYC.

Hord, S., W. Rutherford, L. Huling-Austin, & G. Hall. 1987 *Taking charge of change.* Wash- ington, DC: Association for Supervision and Curriculum Development.

*Individuals with Disabilities Education Act (IDEA) Amendments of 1991. U.S. Statutes at Large* 105: 587-608.

Klein, S.M., E. Tertell, & J. Jewett. 1995. *Best practices in integration—Outreach inservice training model: Teachers' stories about inclusion.* Bloomington: Indiana University.

Klein, S.M., & S. Kontos. 1993. *Best practices in integration inservice training model: In- structional modules and guide.* Bloomington: Indiana University.

Mallory, B.L., & R.S. New. 1994. *Diversity and developmentally appropriate practices: Chal- lenges for early childhood education.* New York: Teachers College Press.

Schön, D. 1983. *The reflective practitioner: How professionals think in action.* New York: Basic.

## Other resources

Ayers, W. 1994 *To teach. The journey of a teacher.* New York: Teachers College Press.

Council for Exceptional Children. *CEC Today.* Ten issues annually. (Council for Exceptional Children, 1920 Association Drive, Reston, VA 20191-1589; 888-232-7733, TTY 703-264-6446; e-mail/editorial: lyndav@cec.sped.org; Website: http://www.cec.sped.org)

Duff, R.E., M.H. Brown, & I.J. Van Scoy. 1995. Reflection and self-evaluation: Keys to professional development. *Young Children* 50 (4): 81–88.

Edwards, C., Forman, G., & Gandini, L. *The hundred languages of children: The Reggio Emilia approach to early childhood education.* New Jersey: Ablex.

Elbow, P. 1986. *Embracing contraries: Explorations in learning and teaching.* New York: Oxford University Press.

Hiemstra, R., & B. Sisco. 1990. *Individualizing instruction: Making learning personal, empowering, and successful.* San Francisco, CA: Jossey-Bass.

Jones, E. 1986. *Teaching adults: An active learning approach.* Washington, DC: NAEYC.

Jones, E. 1993. *Growing teachers: Partnerships in staff development.* Washington, DC: NAEYC.

Jones, E., & J. Nimmo. 1994. *Emergent curriculum.* Washington, DC: NAEYC.

NAEYC, DEC/CEC (Division for Early Childhood of the Council for Exceptional Children), & NBPTS (National Board for Professional Teaching Standards). 1996. *Guidelines for preparation of early childhood professionals.* Washington, DC: NAEYC.

*Seeds of change–Leadership and staff development.* 1996. The Early Childhood Program: A Place to Learn and Grow series. 30 min. Videocassette. Washington, DC: NAEYC.

*Tools for teaching developmentally appropriate practice: The leading edge in early childhood education.* 1998. Produced by Resources and Instruction for Staff Excellence. Set of videocassettes. 180 min. Washington, DC: NAEYC.

Turnbull, H.R., & A.P. Turnbull. 1998. *Free appropriate public education: The law and children with disabilities.* Denver, CO: Love Publishing.

# Play 1

*Sherry Callas, Jane Bruns Mellinger, and Mary King Taylor*

*with Liz Tertell and Jan Jewett as mentors*

Children's lives and learning are full of play. Whether teachers value play or wish to minimize it, they encounter children's playful behaviors and activity hourly. For this reason every teacher needs to understand play and its place in children's lives.

Adults who reflect on their own memories of satisfying play have access to what Freud calls "the royal road" to understanding their own inner life. When adults can apply this understanding to others, they more easily appreciate the importance of play in the development of each young child.

Play is defined as behavior that is self-motivated, freely chosen, process oriented, and pleasurable. In the course of play, children experience freedom, initiative, control, self-expression, movement, and—very importantly—joy. When children play, they are combining new learning with old in ways that are both stimulating and manageable. Again and again, research in children's learning and development confirms the importance of play (Johnson, Christie, & Yawley 1987; Fromberg 1997, 1998).

Ensuring that children have the daily play experiences so beneficial to their development is a key part of the early childhood teacher's job. Thus teachers will find value in reflecting carefully on the nature of children's play and its place in the total learning environment. As teachers we must ask ourselves in what ways we respond to children's play in all the circumstances and variety in which it occurs. The following three teachers reflect on their experiences with and evolving ideas about play.

1

**Sherry Callas** wanted to write about play because she thinks that "play is the most important thing in children's lives." Sherry says, "Something as obvious as play in a child's life isn't as easy to facilitate as it seems." **Jane Bruns Mellinger** wrote about play, she says, "because my ideas and thoughts about the purpose of play and how play fits into the education environment have really evolved since I graduated, mainly through my experiences as a teacher and a parent. I have been able to discover how important play is as a vehicle in learning." **Mary King-Taylor** chose to write about the subject of play because, as she says, "I have rethought play recently. My gut reaction has always been that it is important, but I used to value it as recreation. Now I value play as a learning tool and a basic human need."

*—Liz Tertell and Jan Jewett*

Sherry Callas

W hen I was a child, my younger brother Jeff and I used to play school. We would set up our basement with chalkboard, desks, and tables. We would stay there for hours. I was the teacher, of course, and Jeff the student. Jeff always got *F*s because he never played school the way I thought was right—the sit-at-your-desk, color-the-dittos, and look-at-books way.

I would say, "Mom, Jeff doesn't play right." My teachers never let us get out of our seats, goof around, or play cars, blocks, and other stuff. Mom, with all her wisdom, would answer, "Sherry, Jeff is playing the way he likes to play. He is actually learning a few things at your pretend school."

My brother and I did learn a lot in our make-believe play school in the basement—and the rest of the play that filled our days. Recalling my childhood allows me to think about how children learn through play. But I haven't always been in touch with the importance of play and what it is like to play.

Throughout my own teaching career, I have found that the teacher-controlled instruction I grew up with is like a magnet that keeps dragging me back. I find myself, pegboard in hand, pulling one of my students to the fine-motor area and telling him to create the pattern I've selected. He fusses, says no, then pouts. The magnet pulls me, making me deaf to his communication and closed to his wants and needs. Usually something clicks. I realize the magnet has its hold on me again. I let go. I release the child to learn through his own activity and play. So he goes, explores his environment, and finds his place. I realize it's the comfort in choosing that will let him feel at home in my classroom, our classroom, his classroom.

## Playing in the dirt

As a student teacher in a kindergarten class in Nashville, Indiana, I learned about the importance of choice in the play environment. The value of play wasn't discussed in any of my college textbooks. But I watched and participated in play every day I went to the small Nashville school. The teacher was fabulous—in every curriculum area children learned through play and active involvement.

*Sherry Callas*, B.S., taught elementary-school children for several years. Currently she teaches in a preschool program for children with special needs.

My favorite location in the classroom was the science/sensory area. Every day a different kind of material appeared in a big bin. I remember in particular a day when dirt filled the bin. The children were ecstatic. They couldn't believe they were allowed to play in the dirt. The kindergarten teacher said to me, "Sherry, it's all yours. You can use the dirt one day, a week, an entire month—it's your choice."

Here was my chance to teach while children played in the dirt. I loved it. But then my own past, that old magnet drawing me toward taking charge of the children's activity, was pulling me back. I wasn't opening my mind to all the possibilities. I simply was thinking dirt—you plant things in dirt—that's what we need to do. So the children and I got out our lima beans and shovels, cups and water, and we planted beans. I was about to tell the kindergarten teacher that we were done with the remaining dirt when I looked up and saw Connor filling up different sized cups with dirt and dumping it into a large bucket. I had a revelation: dirt doesn't have to be used only for planting. The children could play in it and learn about measuring. I had made my first step toward breaking out of the mold of setting the whole curriculum in advance. In the end we used the dirt for a month, changing it to mud and then to dirt again; in the process the children and I explored skills in many developmental areas.

One day Connor brought a miniature car over to the dirt bin. Before thinking, I said, "Connor, don't put the car in the dirt; it will get dirty and break." Connor and all the children at the table looked at me, so amazed at my words that I might have been from another planet. I stepped back a moment; a powerful memory took hold of me, and I was a child again:

> "Sherry, hurry up! I can't hold the hose anymore. It's too slippery."
>
> "I've got all the cars, Jeff, just give me a sec." The cars get dumped into a large pile in the center of the flower bed; five kids jump in to grab as many possible.
>
> "Wait a minute," Jeff says. "We have to do this fairly." (Being fair, I remember, was very important to us.)
>
> "We can count them out one car per person."
>
> By then Jeff had dropped the hose, and about two gallons of mud had spilled over the rock edging of the flowerbed—all the better to mud-bog in. Within five minutes, five kids had 12 cars each, except Kim, who had 13, but two were missing wheels so we decided that was OK.

The maps, bridges, and roads we made that day! And I still remember using counting and fractions to solve the problems that came up, doing more real work with math than we kids had ever done. Of course we didn't realize we were actually learning or exploring math concepts—it just happened naturally.

*With all my early childhood experiences in college,
I still did not have a solid understanding of
play. That magnetic pull back to
textbook teaching was hard
to shake as a young
teacher.*

Back in the present. Connor was running the car slowly around the plastic edging of the dirt bin, afraid of getting it dirty. I freed my mind of old habits and grabbed more small cars for Connor and the other children. We made intricate roadways and bridges that day; then to create our own maps, we reproduced our dirt roadways on paper with markers and colored pencils. This day was one of my favorites in teaching.

## Learning from peers in play

With all my early childhood experiences in college, I still did not have a solid understanding of play. That magnetic pull back to textbook teaching was hard to shake as a young teacher. I began working at an institutional facility for children who were visually impaired or blind. I taught a small class of 5- to 7-year-old children whose disabilities ranged from mild mental handicap to severe physical limitation; all were visually impaired or blind as well.

Each day we would start the morning with corner or circle time. The children seemed to like this way of preparing themselves for their work time. The schedule had become so regimented that the children could go through each day on automatic pilot—basically *boring*!

After morning corner time each child received a work tray of various manipulatives such as bolts and screws, boards with pegs and patterns, shape sorters, and beads and patterns. Every day was the same—work, work, work—and what were they learning? After a month I decided to allow some daily time for play. After work-tray time I gave the children about 30 minutes to play before lunch. I started bringing items from home such as old clothes, pots and pans, baby dolls, and unused telephones. We started to play.

One day a few weeks later, Jackie was busying herself making cookies with the playdough and cookie cutters. I heard her ask Leshaun, "Would you like purple cookies or orange cookies?" Leshaun had been unable to identify her colors when drilled with flash cards, but I heard her reply, "I'll take the purple cookies, they're my favorite color!" She had learned her colors in two weeks, mainly through playing with playdough with Jackie.

Jackie was the most social child in my class, welcoming anyone to play with her. I was particularly pleased one day when Mark asked to play with Jackie. Most of the time Mark was withdrawn, restricting himself to a few toys and tabletop activities. With his limited vision, Mark found comfort in those places he knew best. But he listened to Jackie and Leshaun play, sometimes moving away from his comfortable environment to get closer to their play.

When Mark finally asked if he could play, Jackie welcomed him with open arms, and they played in the house area. Mark hadn't yet explored this area, so he took his time to search out all the props. When he found the pretend blender that made a whizzing noise as the button was pushed, it was as if he had struck gold. Mark played in this area continuously for two weeks before following Jackie or Leshaun to other areas. During those two weeks of house playing, Mark learned how to fold clothes, pour liquids, call on the telephone, button a shirt, and zip and snap a jacket. The entire self-help skills area of his IEP (Individualized Education Plan—goals based on the decision of a team of parents, teachers, and therapists) had been completed in two weeks!

Quiet, unsocial Mark became the nonstop talker who wanted to participate in everything. The change was remarkable. One day Mark asked the facility's dorm mom if he could help do the laundry, and she agreed. She was surprised to find that Mark was a great asset in the laundry room. Through his play in the classroom, he had learned how to fold clothes, hang and button shirts, and pour the detergent.

## Taking stock

I started to compare what I observed and noted about the children before and after they had a daily opportunity to play. The difference was remarkable. Before I incorporated play into our schedule, the children's accomplishments were few and slow. After play became a major part of their day, the children accomplished more of their IEP goals and at a faster pace. For example, Allison needed to work on fine-motor skills to prepare her for pre-braille study, and I found that her fine-motor skills had increased noticably. I had to order another Lego set because Allison often used every block in constructing a building and requested more to continue her structure. Using Legos strengthened her hands and her fine-motor coordination.

Allison's spatial perception also improved through play. For example, before play was part of her daily schedule, she rarely moved around the room at more than a slow, tentative walk. Jackie, who had some sight, would initiate active games such as hide-and-seek or tag. Allison was wary at first but eventually developed a passion for these games. Playing these active games, she improved in balance and spatial perception until she was moving at a fast walk, sometimes a run. This ability to move more freely around a room allowed Allison to build her confidence and self-esteem.

As I made more and more time for play, our designated "work time" was becoming shorter and shorter. One day I realized our morning corner or circle time had become more interactive, with us

all—children and teacher—more comfortable in discussing the daily schedule and our lives. Social play had increased the children's confidence and their ability to communicate verbally and nonverbally.

## Teaching that supports play

When I became a facilitator for children who were visually impaired, I had further opportunities to learn to guide children's play. By providing the right tools and playing a part in the drama of play, I learned to teach naturalistically, using strategies I knew from my special education training, such as verbal prompts and incidental and time-delay procedures. Time delay allows students to teach each other and lets the child with less knowledge relating to the question at hand reflect on the problem and draw her own conclusions.

For example, when Ryan asked, "Do all planes have 10 rows of seats?" I waited a moment before answering, looking around the group of children with a questioning expression. Karen spoke up and said, "The plane Mom and I were on had lots and lots of rows. I think Mom called it a Boeing 747. It was huge!" Jacob popped up, saying, "In my Richard Scarry book the airplanes are all different sizes and shapes." After questions about sizes and shapes and uses for airplanes started spilling forth from the children, the kindergarten teacher and I arranged a class field trip to the airport. The children loved the experience, which helped to answer many of their questions.

Teaching in the play context enabled me to broaden the children's problem-solving abilities as well as their divergent thinking. I learned that I could facilitate the children's successful completion of tasks by providing support, focused attention, physical proximity, and verbal encouragement. I saw children learning by trial and error, and I learned that their conceptions as well as their misconceptions reflect their developing ideas and thoughts.

Looking back, I realize that I developed new teaching roles. I planned activities, schedules, and arrangements. I set up and modified the environment. I became a supporter of relationships among children as well as an assessor of their progress. The roles of the teacher are just as important when education has a strong play component and an emphasis on social interaction.

Instead of managing and controlling children's learning all day, the adult often has to facilitate. Facilitating sometimes means supporting relationships among children during play. Facilitating can be quite straightforward or very complex. I experienced a complex problem with a relationship when two children who were good friends became exclusive, isolating themselves from other children. As a facilitator, I wanted to help Terry and Margie open up and include other children in their play. Taking into account the concerns of the girls' parents, I decided on an intervention I thought might help. Terry and Margie particularly enjoyed playing in the art area, so I expanded the physical space for art activities to accommodate five children rather than two. The activities I chose to put in the art area were cooperative activities such as murals or papier-mâché.

After a while Margie began to share activities with other children, thus expanding her social environment. With Terry I needed to consider further strategies. Developmentally advanced in imagination and intelligence, she asked lots of questions, always seeking knowledge and understanding. I used this characteristic of Terry's to create bridges in her social play. When she started expressing interest in a few of the older children in the class, I decided to involve her in a small-group activity with them —making brownies.

As I set out the materials, ingredients, and equipment, I asked the children questions such as, "Why do we need the measuring cups?" Sam replied, "Is it because we don't want to ruin the brownies by putting too much stuff in them?" Then Terry asked, "Why do brownies always get chewy?" Sam answered, "That's because your mom puts too much rubber in them." Everybody laughed, and Terry said, "Oh, stop! Anyway, my dad is the one who puts too much rubber in them." The laughter continued as we played word games giving every silly name we could to each brownie. Terry's social realm grew that day, over a plate of brownies.

## Play and the child with special needs

As lead teacher at a developmental learning center, I gained a deeper understanding of how play promotes the development of children with special needs. I had three preschoolers with special needs in my class.

Aaron, a child with moderate to severe cerebral palsy, was 3 years old. He liked to look at Richard Scarry books, play with miniature cars, and listen to the storybook *Jam Berry* on tape. An energetic and happy boy, Aaron had limited mobility. He could crawl, using his arms and one leg. He needed assistance to eat and sometimes to move around the room. These special needs did not interfere with his work. He played in every area of our classroom, including dramatic play. He had several good friends and was always included in the fun.

One morning, Aaron crawled to the block area where he found the cars and wooden blocks. He looked for his favorite car, found it, and proceeded to drive it up a ramp. Jeffrey, a typically developing peer, looked over to his friend and realized Aaron couldn't reach the top of the platform that the rest of the children had built. Without adult prompting and being careful not to tip the entire structure, Jeffrey removed some blocks to lower the platform to Aaron's eye level. Aaron smiled his appreciation and continued his travel along the longest part of the structure. The two boys drove cars and rammed them into each other's for quite some time until I noticed that Aaron had enlarged the radius of his play circle by six feet. This was the farthest Aaron had ever crawled in the time I had known him. The rapport Aaron and Jeffrey had established empowered them as learners, doers, and creators. Jeffrey's and Aaron's learning was an engaging, interactive process that changed from day to day.

The block area wasn't the only area in which Aaron could be involved without adult assistance. With the aid of a stander, Aaron enjoyed the sensory activity table. He would stand for hours playing in the sand, water, salt, coffee, wood chips, or gravel. Using a variety of objects, such as cups and spoons, small animals, large animals, cars, boats, shovels, or any other items offered, Aaron would socialize, share objects, cooperate, and play with his friends.

One day Cliff, who has autism, chose the painting area to play in. He and Robert, a child with delayed speech, actively exchanged fingerpaints, managing to paint the entire table, floor, walls, and themselves in the process. I was delighted! Cliff, whose special needs made it more difficult for him to socialize with others, had made a connection with another child. Robert and Cliff didn't need to talk, yet they had a social experience. They painted until they were both exhausted. The experience was remarkable! Through play, these children with special needs experienced fewer environmental limits, participated with their peers, and developed at their own pace.

Before my experience at the developmental learning center, I thought that children with special needs needed special classes, separate from the early childhood classroom where typically developing children were enrolled. During my work at the center, I learned differently: as children play, they enter a world in which each child, whatever her needs and abilities, is able to learn and develop to her own potential.

## Creating possibilities

One place where that recurring magnetic force—the tendency to overdirect—rarely takes hold of teachers, no matter what their educational ideas, is the outdoor play area. For most teachers that role falls off at the door like a discarded book bag. Outdoors with young children, teachers are captured by play. Even as a directive teacher I used to play with the children outdoors. I didn't think of that time as education. I was so wrong. I came to this conclusion one sunny day while sitting under the school playground's elevated tree house structure.

Cassie, Terry, Jacob, Margie, and I were busy with shovels pretending to make cakes out of the dirt. We described in detail the elegant cakes with chocolate icing and pink rosebuds made out of fallen leaves. Our enterprise increased our descriptive vocabulary with words such as *pastry, chef,* and *scones.* I drew on my knowledge from the bakery shop I walked by every day on the way to work. Like the scent from the fresh, hot cinnamon rolls I sometimes bought for breakfast, word images of a bakery wafted from my mouth.

The children and I moved to the sandbox, collecting the necessary utensils for creating our own bakery. Each child was busily fashioning his or her own masterpiece. Jacob, a child whose family had recently emigrated from Italy, said, "I am making bread like my grandma makes. It's so good!" Margie said, "I want to make bread too, but I need a pan." I responded, "Margie, how about that red bucket with the broken handle. It looks like a bread pan to me." She smiled and said, "Perfect-amondo." Everyone laughed and eagerly continued to create baked goods.

Our work as teachers doesn't have to be restricted to the curriculum inside four walls, I was learning. We can enhance children's lives beyond, using the natural world as a learning environment. I began to bring out materials that could enhance the play of the children and adults. One day I created new possibilities with four empty boxes. I lined them up in a row, stepped back, and let the children "fill in the blanks." They decided to make the four boxes a train, jumping inside, sounding the bell, and moving into a fantasy world of train rides. A few empty boxes had opened up a place where the children could play for hours, changing the boxes from train car to tower to roller coaster. The only boundaries to the possibilities were those the children made. In the outdoors most teachers step back a little, let go of some of the structure, and allow children to be more free. But we can do this indoors too.

Outdoor play reminds me of a particular time when I was about 5 years old.

One cloudy day I heard a quiet, urgent voice from over the fence: "Come and see what I made. It's a secret!"

My playmate Kim pointed to a stand of pine trees. Pretending we were soldiers, crouching as we made our way across an open field so as not to be spotted, we took cover in the pines.

"Don't tell anyone about this, not even Jeff," said Kim. "It can be our little secret."

I quickly agreed and peeked through the pines. Where browning pine needles had been only a few days earlier, I now saw a space maybe five feet square and two feet deep, where the black earth had been carved out to create three seats. An old milk crate resembling a table was located in the center.

Fascinated and impressed, I stepped down into the secret place. "It took me two days to dig," Kim admitted, "but isn't it great?"

"Yeah, it's wonderful!" I replied. "Can we play in it now?"

I chose to be the Lion from *The Lion, the Witch, and the Wardrobe*—powerful and caring. Kim was a bird. "I'd like to fly and find mysterious things, pick them up, and travel home here to my nest," she said.

We played for months, using the small secret place dug out of the earth. It housed a whole world of make-believe—fairy-tale romances, wars, neighborhood drive-ins, soda shops, schoolhouses, and grocery stores. The time spent mapping out strategies, building tents to keep

out the elements, and organizing our complex world helped us grow cognitively and socially in a great many ways.

Children's favorite play spaces are places such as tight, angular corners between walls and couches, a pile of dirt, a puddle, a hole, a perch to climb to, or even a spot where plaster is chipping away and beckons small fingers. As teachers we find ourselves confronting our adult instincts for order, function, cleanliness, and safety, trying to work out compromises and trade-offs. We continually seek to balance children's and adults' needs, safety and risk, challenge and convenience, freedom and independence.

## Play and social support

As I reflect on my years teaching in South Bend, Indiana, I remember one day in our play-based special needs classroom. Ben came to school—quiet and shy, he had never been away from his mother for very long. However, he quickly made a place for himself among the many toys and activity centers, favoring the sensory "pool" with its variety of textures and sensations. He moved play people and miniature cars through the pool's contents, sometimes burrowing himself to make a bed or a trail for his play characters to follow. Every day he looked forward to the sensory pool.

A big step in Ben's development came the day he took Jacob by the hand and led him to the sensory pool. Neither child had developed verbal skills, but Jacob, a very social child with special needs, came along willingly. Ben lined up golf balls along the edge of the pool and offered Jacob the tongs for picking them up. Jacob was fairly good at accomplishing the squeezing motion, and when he finished his turn, he passed the tongs to Ben. This sharing went on until the game was mastered, and from that day forward Ben and Jacob were friends.

Because of his sociability, Jacob engaged many people in his play. A notable experience included the day a group of kindergartners came as volunteers into our special needs class, eager to join in my children's play. One kindergartner "read" a book Jacob held out to her, telling the story her way, and giving it an even better ending. Immediately Jacob jumped up to bring another book. After a time the kindergartner led Jacob to the tabletop toy area where they played together, with the kindergartner completing any tasks too difficult for Jacob. The attention made Jacob happy. The play helped the kindergartners develop many skills as they showed the preschoolers what to do.

I know I am still learning what play contributes to children's development, through all my experiences and in my struggle against that magnetic pull of teacher-controlled instruction.

# Sherry's mentors reflect . . .

Sherry is fortunate in having access to satisfying memories of her own play as a child and the contributions it made to her growth and development. Thinking back to these experiences has helped her see the many skills and understandings that play develops. This awareness has enabled her to become effective and confident in supporting play and explaining its value to others who may not remember or connect to their own childhood play.

Satisfaction and mastery are evident in the play situation that Sherry recounts between Cliff and Robert. Adults, too, benefit from opportunities to be spontaneous and creative—to play. Through the richness of their own experiences, they bring confidence, appreciation, and creativity to the children whose play they are supporting.

Choice and control are essential in play; they are what give children such intense satisfaction in play. This presents a dilemma for teachers who feel responsible for children's learning. Sherry's description of Mark's behavior illustrates how play tends to occur in stages. First, children explore their environment, including the people, the place, and the materials. They do this by interacting with these things or by observing closely, often while others are interacting. Then as children are comfortable and familiar with the environment, they begin to interact, experiment, and manipulate.

Once children gain confidence in being able to predict and control their interactions, the playful quality and creative possibilities increase. Mastery is the exciting outcome of this play process. Children integrate their learning, mastering interactions with people and things in their environment. The sense of confidence and joy that children experience in play gives them the energy and interest to start new explorations and take on new challenges. Mark exercises mastery gained in the house corner as he becomes the dorm mother's helper and gains a satisfying relationship through his new skills. In ways such as these, play nurtures growth and progress.

In a curriculum that takes play seriously, educators face a question not always easy to answer: When should one stand back and when should one take action to extend and enrich children's play and development? Sherry is working on the various roles she assumes in children's learning and development, developing her skills in expanding the art of teaching.

In Sherry's description of Ben's entry into play, we see certain familiar steps—first the careful exploring, manipulating, and mastering of the sensory pool and then the taking of a social risk that leads to a major accomplishment. Ben initiates a friendship. This friendship, in turn, will enhance Ben's play experiences and contribute to his ongoing development. In this instance Sherry made a decision to stand back and observe. But she had created the environment that allowed children the time and control to develop play skills as well as relationships.

Recall play experiences from your childhood. What types of games did you play? What types of play were the most interesting to you? Least interesting? Think about your own classroom (or one you have observed extensively). What types of play get the most support in this program? Which get the least?

Think about "magnets" from your past that still have a pull on you. What are some real-life constraints (for example, schedules, materials, class size) that limit play in your classroom? Brainstorm a few possible solutions.

Think of yourself in the following roles in children's play: observer, player, instructor, facilitator. In which roles are you most comfortable? Least comfortable? Design a plan for working on the role or roles in which you are least comfortable.

What words come to mind when you think of children playing outdoors? Now how about children playing indoors? What differences and similarities do you notice in the two sets of words?

# Jane Bruns Mellinger

Jane Bruns Mellinger

That children do much of their most important learning through play is not a concept I have always understood. My early educational training was in the field of elementary and special education. The elementary field places a heavy emphasis on direct instruction and rote learning. In the past, special education largely emphasized a deficit model of remediation. The focus was on teaching to an individual's strengths to redress the deficits, which meant that we only worked on deficits—what children didn't know, what they couldn't do.

In my college training the message was that if you listen, learn, and arm yourself with the tools your courses give you, then you will be a competent, successful teacher. We came away with the idea that we should follow the directions exactly. If we did, the magic formula would work. (*Caution!* Do not deviate from the plan; at all costs follow the plan.) Of course, it didn't take long for me or others to discover that there is no such thing as a magic formula.

The tools with which I entered teaching were just that—simply tools, some useful, some less so. The philosophy of education I had been taught, the teaching techniques, and the methods were a very limited menu from which to select. I had been given, at best, a starter set of blocks that I would continually need to add to and change.

In 1988 I had a challenging experience that was a significant turning point for me as an educator. Entering an early childhood special education program, I soon discovered that my old set of blocks no longer would work. And as I examined assumptions and beliefs, I soon realized that I had started acquiring them not in college but very early in my life.

I am the oldest of six sisters in a close-knit family. My father worked long, hard hours throughout my childhood. My mother worked at home. Living on a farm, we all were responsible for farm chores as well as regular housework. Summertime was not a vacation from work and responsibility at home. On the farm, play was something we could do after the work was done. The work, the chores, the

*Jane Bruns Mellinger, M.S., has worked with individuals with disabilities and their families as a teacher, consultant, and administrator. Currently she serves as director of the Anthony Wayne Infant and Toddler Services in Indianapolis, Indiana.*

responsibility were foremost; play was a bonus or reward for work well done. Play was valued as special, in the same way as were family vacations or outings. As a beginning teacher, I carried these values into my classroom in the way I emphasized academics and formal learning. Even though I tried to make learning fun, free time and play were something I allowed only after the work or assignments were completed.

*On the farm, play was something we could do after the work was done . . . a bonus or reward for work well done.*

## Rediscovering play

Then I entered the field of early childhood special education, and many of my previous conceptions, practices, and beliefs were challenged over the next several years. These challenges were to come from children—my own 4-year-old son and the children I taught—as well as from my studies.

This was my first experience of total immersion in early childhood education, specifically early intervention for ages 3 to 5. Initially I was hired as a teacher for preschool children with special needs. At that time a pilot program was being implemented in the public school system in anticipation of passage of a federal law (Public Law 99-457) mandating preschool services to children with disabilities beginning at age 3. Our pilot included children with special needs in community preschools serving all children rather than in settings only for children with disabilities.

My supervisor instructed me to prepare lessons and activities for a one-on-one instructional session with each child in my caseload. Specific goals and objectives were written for each child, and these were very academic in nature. The activities were planned to provide direct teaching to the preschool child to remediate deficit areas identified through assessment. This instruction was to be provided in a one-hour, pull-out session, that is, the child was taken out of the classroom, often alone.

I prepared my "lessons," packed my bag, and went to work. Each lesson was to focus on one concept or skill such as color recognition or identification, number concepts, one-to-one correspondence, prepositional concepts, and answering *who, what, when,* and *where* questions. Although I had used this approach in the past, I soon became frustrated using it with these preschoolers. They really weren't interested, and I could understand why! They wanted to play, to interact, to explore, and they weren't especially interested in doing pencil-and-paper tasks or learning letters and numbers, at least not in the out-of-context way I was teaching them!

Jason is a good example. When I first began working with him, he was 3 years old. Jason has Down syndrome and developmental delays in all areas, but he has a joyful personality. I began my initial interventions with Jason at his home in a one-on-one instructional session. I brought materials with me to teach Jason color recognition, one-to-one correspondence, the concepts of "boy" and "girl," and basic prepositions such as *under, over, beside, behind, on top of,* and *in front of.* I chose materials that I thought would appeal to him, but his attention and interest were low. *He* wanted to be in control. *He* wanted to direct his own learning. Because I was doing tasks he didn't want to do, he reacted by acting silly and trying my patience. When I changed my approach a bit and looked for teachable moments in his play, he did learn some concepts and skills along the way. I thought I was so clever for sneaking learning into Jason's play! I was beginning to catch on, but I still had a long way to go. For example, I still tried to keep Jason in a chair as we worked. Because I was teaching, I thought the child needed to sit and be attentive. But it wasn't working. Soon I realized that it made more sense to sit on the floor for most activities. Also, moving about and doing activities worked better.

## The play context

I began to worry if all this interaction was really working. How could my activities with Jason, taught in isolation, carry over to the classroom and real life? I began experimenting by working with a child within the regular preschool classroom and the activities taking place there. For example, it made sense for children to practice cutting in the context of classroom activities instead of having them cut pieces of paper for no reason other than to master the skill.

I discovered that many goals I was supposed to be working on with children could easily be introduced within the context of classroom activities and play. An excellent example is turn taking. This skill was so much easier to teach—and more relevant—in the context of a group game of sharing limited materials than in a one-on-one adult-child instructional session. Turn taking begins to makes sense to children when one child really wants her turn and everyone else does too. Involving children's peers in activities became quite natural.

I began to see that other children often were more effective teachers or models for a child with special needs than I was. One day I was in the classroom watching Mike struggle with the playdough that the children were making from a recipe. Mike's playdough was an oozing glob. Sam, a 5-year-old working nearby, turned his attention to Mike and explained the need for more dry stuff to take away the "smushyness." With Sam's assistance, Mike added more flour and more salt, and he had workable dough.

Everyone gained from this experience. I learned how important peers are. Sam was able to explain a process and suggest a method that worked, and he enjoyed being the expert and helping someone. Mike not only learned the process of mixing and of physical changes but also had the very positive experience of learning from and interacting with a peer. Mike's family had been concerned that the children would not include him in the classroom or that he wouldn't make friends, yet he became a very important class member—his name was often first on the list of birthday guests. None of this would have happened if I had continued to pull him out separately for his lessons. He truly became a player in this community.

## Gaining confidence in the payoff of play

I became more and more interested in the field of early childhood education and began a lot of reading as well as attending workshops and training. With each new learning experience, I slowly reshaped my approach to education. Instead of taking complete charge of children's instruction and learning, I gave more thought to creating an environment that was inviting and conducive to interaction and involvement. Gradually I began to share control, allowing the children to initiate their own learning and capitalizing upon their interests. I became more skilled at facilitating children's learning and development by seizing the teachable moments and building upon children's natural interests.

My supervisor at the time was firmly entrenched in the concept of direct instruction and remediation and vehemently opposed to play and children's natural activities as the context for learning. The approach I was beginning to embrace was difficult to grasp and adhere to. With me the process began when I faced the fact that the methods I was using were flawed. For any of us, it is not easy to admit that what we have always done may not be best for children. To persevere in a faulty method, however, simply because we are unable to admit a mistake is to do a great injustice. Admitting our mistakes is never easy, nor is change.

I realize that most people, including families and teachers, want their children to succeed in school. I see that sometimes it is easier to evaluate systematic instruction and rote learning ("I taught *red,* that's how I know he knows it"). I have learned to acknowledge these needs and our fears of not meeting them. We all want children to reach their potentials. Since I want to share these views of children's learning with others, I am searching for ways to show them how much stronger, richer, and deeper learning and development are in a play context.

For me, the whole idea of learning through play and peer interaction began to make more and more sense, and as I experimented with this approach, I found that it was much more effective than my one-on-one, direct-instruction model. Further, as the children worked and played together, they were becoming more socially competent. And I was able to provide assistance naturally to the children in situations relevant to each child.

## Working at play

Supporting children's learning in the context of play was, I discovered, a skill that did not come to me naturally. I had to work at it, probably because of the way that I was raised and the type of educational philosophy emphasized in my college experience. To make matters worse, I found myself in the awkward position of not only trying to change my own thinking and teaching methods but also having to defend my new approaches to others. The value of play in children's learning can be difficult to explain to those who adhere to more traditional methods of direct instruction. Being rather unsure at

first of my own thinking and beliefs about these ways of teaching and learning, which were in the process of change, made it very hard for me to explain the approach to others. Even more difficult was trying to convince proponents of direct teaching and drill on isolated skills that young children do not learn well this way.

Many educators, including those in the field of traditional special education, have strong feelings that children with special needs require more direct instruction than do their typical peers so as to improve deficit areas. I have often seen territorial belief that only those trained in special education have the skills and expertise to teach children with special needs.

As I began to read more widely, take advantage of different kinds of training available in the field, and continue my quest for knowledge and growth, I decided to pursue additional certification in early childhood special education. I fortunately encountered several wonderful mentors along the way who taught me much. These mentors included children as well as adults! The more I learned, the more I wanted to know and the more reflective I became.

My education foundation is stronger now. I know how to help others reflect on and work toward change. I can answer questions about play and how children learn best. I no longer have any doubts: we all learn better, more effectively, when what we are learning is relevant, when we have some control and interest. The teacher is important, very important. The teacher observes children closely and considers what experiences and kinds of learning the children—as a group and individually—are ready for. Arranging the environment, providing materials, and interacting with the children in a variety of ways, the teacher supports their learning and development.

## Play and inclusion

In 1991 special education classes for all preschoolers with special needs were mandated in Indiana. Our pilot program serving 70 to 75 children expanded quickly. The school system's administration initially decided to pull back from neighborhood program involvement and provide self-contained classes within the school system. There were many pros and cons in this difficult administrative decision. One of the most negative effects of this decision was elimination of opportunity for children with special needs to interact with typically developing peers. Our center-based special education preschool classrooms educated eight preschool children with special needs in a classroom with a teacher and a classroom assistant. It quickly became apparent to me that the missing component—children with the full range of abilities—made quite a difference. Adults could facilitate learning and play, but the stimulation of other children, their play skills and language, could not be duplicated by the adults. This essential stimulation seemed sorely missing in some classrooms. Fortunately our administration agreed and began to integrate children with special needs with their typically developing peers.

Many changes have occurred in our program since the passage of special needs legislation. By the fall of 1995, Indiana had many preschoolers with special needs fully included in community preschools. All our center-based preschool programs now include children with special needs with typically developing peers. I see their inclusion as a critical element in all children's development of social competence and play skills and thus essential to their optimal development and learning.

## Reflecting on changing views

*I no longer have any doubts: we all learn better, more effectively, when what we are learning is relevant, when we have some control and interest.*

Through my personal journey of change, I have learned and grown. I know that when we offer rich and stimulating experiences, children are wonderful choreographers of their own learning, whether alone, in pairs, or in small or large groups. All children have much to give and receive from one another. I have changed my role as a teacher. I observe, facilitate, stimulate, and provide for children the opportunities to explore and experiment. With practice I will become more proficient in assisting and gently guiding children's learning rather than insistently controlling and directing this learning. When children's individual interests are taken into account, their learning becomes so much richer, more meaningful, and personally relevant to each child.

While I have changed my own philosophy of education, many of my fellow teachers, both in our center-based preschool programs and in community preschools, are not in agreement. I recognize their concerns and know that we all want children to succeed. I will continue to advocate for the approach that includes play, but I know this change in me was a gradual process.

Some of my colleagues will make a similar, often painful journey, just as I will continue to evolve as an educator. It is *never* easy to admit one's mistakes; it is *never* easy to change oneself.

# Jane's mentors reflect . . .

At first Jane set out to instruct children such as Jason in the concepts she wanted to teach and decide when and how she wanted to teach them. It didn't work. She began to see that children have other ways of learning. In play they have greater control. They focus on the aspects of the situation that interest them; they use and stretch the capacities that are just emerging; and they manage the pace, the repetitiveness, and the scope of the activity.

Jane had to look at her own values and beliefs about play and learning. Like many of us, she grew up in a culture that values work and sees play only as a reward for hard work. As Jane recognizes, teachers have a tendency to give children tasks that they see as real work and then to reward them with play time. While play is natural and pleasurable for children, it is not necessarily easy. Children debate, negotiate, question, and challenge one another in their play. They explore, solve problems, and experiment. Their learning through play is often more complex and impressive than what they learn through other means, and their strong motivation makes this possible.

I am impressed with Jane's ability to let go of her need to control interactions. She says that seeing children learn and make progress through play helped her to do this. Looking at how she had acquired her assumptions and beliefs about learning, teaching, work, and play was also important. We each must consider carefully what will help us to relax our need to be in control. Then we can nurture and engage in the spontaneous and creative processes that make play so worthwhile.

As she gives the children more play opportunities, Jane sees the important contributions that peers make in the learning process. Her growing awareness of this dynamic also helps her to share the control and responsibility for learning. Because children are at different developmental levels and because they have differing areas of expertise and varied interests, they can learn a lot from each other. Playing with others is a comfortable and meaningful way to learn. For example, Mike gained new knowledge and skills from his interactions with Sam. The interactions were meaningful for Sam too, as he clarified his own knowledge in trying to explain to someone else. We are learning more and more about how valuable it is for children to have the opportunity to interact with a variety of peers and how groups heterogeneous by age, abilities, and other characteristics are beneficial to all.

Think about the values your family had about work, play, and learning. How did you learn about these values? Were they spoken or implied? How do these values affect you and your classroom philosophy today?

Create your own commercial or public service announcement for play. Think about what things are most important for other adults to know about learning through play.

Your thoughts about how children learn and develop have probably changed over the years. Think back to significant changes that took place in your thinking—from your own childhood and adolescence through your various educational and work experiences to the present. You may want to put them on a timeline.

Sometimes a given activity can be play or work depending on how it's approached. Think about a time when something you thought would be play for you became work. How did it make you feel?

Think of a metaphor to describe play in your classroom or a classroom with which you are familiar. Share and compare these ideas with others.

# Mary King-Taylor

W hen I studied theories of child development in undergraduate school, for me they were interesting but without application to the real world. Working in a state institution as a strict behaviorist, I thought that everything was learned through reward and punishment in drilled lessons. Most of the mental retardation literature I read in professional journals supported this view. I gave little thought to educating people to think, only training people to do specific tasks.

In graduate school I studied the uniqueness of various handicapping conditions, along with learning more about behaviorist-oriented approaches. By then the field was changing. Reformers stressed the importance of enabling people to be successful in communities. We needed to teach personal management, adaptive behavior, social skills, and vocational skills. My curriculum reflected those objectives, but my approach was still that of a human behaviorist. I improved my behavior management techniques and gave more weight to intrinsic rewards, striving for generalization of skills to real situations. I considered personal preferences, dislikes, and more effective schedules of rewards. I continued to follow basic behaviorism.

A year ago I was asked about my theory of how children learn. To my surprise I found myself at a loss for words. I could describe the usual progression of skills and how to teach specific behavioral skills, but I did not have an overall theory of how children learn. I was embarrassed but determined to resolve my shortcomings. First I was introduced to the reasoning behind the "developmentally appropriate" philosophy that is central to early childhood education. Through reflection on constructivist theories of development, curriculum, and the Best Practices Project, I began to formulate my view on how children learn and develop the ability to think for themselves. I was introduced to the major role that play has in the development of all thinking human beings. Some years ago I had taken a play therapy course, and the professor told us again and again, "Play is the work of childhood." Until recently I didn't realize the force of his statement.

**Mary King-Taylor**, M.A., has worked with children and adults with special needs in public schools, state institutions, and child protective services and most recently in an inclusive K–2 classroom.

## Starting to consider play

At the beginning of my career in
working with individuals with developmental delays, I viewed play as something to
pass the time and add enjoyment to life. Those who
lived in the institutions where I worked often sat around
large, empty wards all day with no worthwhile use of their time.
Giving them play opportunities seemed like a good idea.

Starting to buy toys and things for children to play with, I had to
think about which play items might interest persons whose developmental level was far below their chronological age. I purchased structured materials: blocks, dolls, rattles, stacking rings, and balls. Each
material had a specific use that I dutifully taught. The materials were
available only for short periods of time when there were enough staff
members to provide close supervision so that children would not
choke on, chew up, or destroy the toys by inappropriately playing
with them. Each child had a specific play goal such as put six rings on
the post without mouthing them.

Using play only as a medium for eliciting desired behaviors, I was
missing the point. And like many teachers, I was using play as a
reward for completing required tasks. I totally overlooked the natural
purpose of play and the benefits it offers.

## Materials and room arrangement

Coming to understand how children learn best has changed what I
do in my classroom. For instance, taking a look at my classroom, I
saw the walls lined with cabinets and holding all my instructional
equipment, with the center of the room reserved as open space for
gross-motor activities and therapy. We got a new student whose
special needs required a quiet area for retreat, so I rearranged the
room to create a small comfortable area for him. As I began to rearrange my room, I had many thoughts. For children to play spontane-
ously, I saw, toys must be where they can be reached. I saw that
children tended to play less with toys not in plain view. I changed the
way I used the cabinets and bookshelves in the room. On lower
shelves I put toys most appealing to the crawler. On middle shelves I
put toys that appealed to a child using a wheelchair. On top shelves I
placed some books and toys of interest to the mobile child. I filled one
side of a bookcase with a variety of toys of interest to children whose
sensory-motor stage requires very close supervision. With these
changes, all my students had access to appropriate toys.

The rearrangement improved children's access to play materials
but created new problems. I always thought that my classroom should

appear neat and orderly to adults, but now toys often are scattered all over the room. I am continually rearranging and changing toys and furniture to accommodate the changing interests and needs of the children. Due to children's differing developmental levels, we must be careful to keep the room safe and functional for all. Sometimes this is especially challenging. For example, I have a student with pica—eating of inappropriate substances such as newspaper, chalk, clay, or paint— yet I want the other children to benefit from having access to art materials, small manipulatives, and related materials. I don't want to keep the child away from peers. The only solution is for classroom staff to be always observant, adaptive, and facilitative.

At the moment I am using the cabinets to house small manipula- tives but keeping the doors open. I encourage children to get into the cabinets, take out materials they want, and return them when they are finished. In the past I just gave each child her materials; now I observe the children's interests and facilitate engaging them in an activity.

Denver frequently gets out toys for himself, and occasionally he also will put a toy on Audrey's desk for her to play with. Neither child talks to the other, but they communicate through this type of sharing. Each child looks out for the other at a distance, being certain to summon help if he or she needs attention. The two demonstrate a level of social awareness that I had not known they had. Before my changes, children sat at their assigned seats and received one-on-one assignments and direction. New spacing and the rearrangement of the room encouraged interactions of this type.

I am still getting lots of stuff for children's play. The difference now is that I am being less of a dictator about how the materials are used.

## Making time to play

Two years ago a colleague told me that she would not like to be a student in my room because there was too much paperwork and not enough fun. I examined my practices and saw that she was right. I ran my class with little or no time set aside for play. My classroom sched- ule was filled with academics taught through drill and practice, using manipulatives. Children were instructed on sorting and matching items in a context of "work." As a recess I gave my students a limited choice of specific games or activities in which they could participate, with age-equivalent peers acting as peer tutors. After recess students completed school jobs and then had lunch. Lunch served as a time for instruction as well as eating. After lunch the students completed necessary grooming and went to the gym for exercise. A half hour of free time followed.

What children are working on and learning hasn't changed much, but children now choose their own activities to meet their work goals.

They spend much less time waiting for turns and more time playing. I let the children show me what they are interested in sorting and matching, and sorting and matching often occur naturally at times like cleanup. Meaningful whole-language activities have added to the enjoyment of learning reading and writing skills. The children seem naturally interested in printing and creating.

I learned to trust the children to know what they want to learn, and I facilitate their doing so. Worksheets are still used at times but far less often. My class materials are more interactive because I let students use them in a range of ways, and the children are more engaged and motivated. Most of all, I have learned that children really are learning while they are playing. This understanding gave me the encouragement to change the schedule of the day.

Making time for play is an issue with which I continually struggle. Academic skills, therapy goals, toileting, feeding—all these things are important, but they seem to compete for time. In addition to meeting these needs, I must work around the administrative constraints of the classroom and school. Our two brief recess periods from 10:15 to 10:30 A.M. and from 1:00 to 1:20 P.M. are the only opportunities my children have to play outdoors. Lunch is served at 11:00 A.M. and must be finished by 11:45. At least half of my students need assistance with toileting on a regular schedule during the day. At designated times on designated days, the children go to music, physical therapy, occupational therapy, gym, swimming, and speech therapy. Each child spends only 50% of his school day, or slightly more, in the classroom. This obviously means that play, therapies, and what I'm used to thinking of as academics must be intertwined.

Having integrated therapies would add a lot more time for learning through play. In an integrated therapy model, therapists work in the classroom to provide services to children within their natural setting. Teachers and therapists work together to plan and implement a play-based curriculum that works on the many goals teachers have for children. The therapist is in the classroom providing services through whatever activity the child is involved in; for example, physical therapy may involve learning to move to a wheelchair from any place in the environment or just moving about in the classroom. An occupational therapist may work with children to improve fine-motor grasp while they are playing, drawing, or eating. Speech-and-language therapy for a given child happens whenever and wherever it may occur—for example, in the course of a game with a small group or through a child's dictating a story to the therapist. In using this approach, the therapist would not pull students away from activities for private therapy, and the child would have more time to play. With an integrated therapy model, I would have more consultation time with

other service providers
and thus be more aware of
therapeutic techniques for enhancing the quality of children's
experiences. This model could help
produce a more productive class schedule.

*I believe that children learn through play, but trust-*
*ing this process is not always easy. I often need*
*to remind myself to let the children figure*
*out things for themselves instead of*
*giving them my solution*
*to their problems.*

## Trusting children's learning

I believe that children learn through play, but trusting this
process is not always easy. I often need to remind myself to let the
children figure out things for themselves instead of giving them my
solution to their problems. When I resist the temptation to help, I am
often amazed at the solutions children suggest for problems, because
they think differently than I do.

For example, Monroe was very upset on his first day in our class.
He stayed in the hall crying for a few minutes. Whenever a staff
member tried to talk to Monroe, he wailed even more loudly. Then
one of the children, Leon, took a keyboard to the doorway of the room
and showed it to Monroe. Monroe started talking to Leon, who still
had the keyboard, and then joined him in hitting the keyboard. Soon
both boys were inside the classroom and playing. Later another child
explained to me that Monroe hadn't believed we had toys that he
could actually play with.

This event had an impact on me in two ways. First, I had been
unaware of Leon's problem-solving skills and of his sensitivity to other
people's feelings. This occasion was the first time I had witnessed
Leon take the initiative to soothe another person. In the past I would
have intervened so promptly that I would never have seen how capable Leon was. Second, I saw that to feel emotionally ready to learn
Monroe needed the sense of security that children find in play.

The day of Monroe's distress gave me another insight. I knew
Monroe at one time had been an unhappy child, crying for hours at a
time, and then in his class two years ago, he was a happy student. I
thought it was because Monroe loved that teacher, but now I could see
that it was more than just their rapport. This teacher communicated
with him and provided the type of learning environment that met his
interests and needs.

## Supporting children's play

Sometimes I take a more active role in children's play. Denver
would lie on the floor lining up cars to create a congested highway.
Left alone, he was happy to do this for hours. He didn't vary the

activity or talk to anyone else when he was playing with his cars. I began to play with Denver and his cars, looking to see if his play could be extended in interesting ways. Now through his play with cars he enjoys counting, is learning his colors, and demonstrates basic concepts of *first, last, big,* and *small.* He has been working on concepts such as *addition* and *comparatives.* He frequently asks questions and solves problems as he plays. He is involved now in building garages, homes, and streets for the cars, and in the process he plans, organizes, and thinks about directions, size, and shape. Denver taught me how much was to be gained by connecting with a child's interests. Still, it is always a challenge to distinguish when I am interfering with a child's play and when I am guiding a child to higher levels of play.

I am getting over my fear of giving children too much time to play. I was having a great deal of difficulty with Bob, a child with autism. He wanted just to lie on a beanbag and watch others. Whenever I imposed academic demands on him, he resisted. A specialist in autism recommended that I not make demands on him unless it was absolutely necessary. Angry and hurt, I thought, "Fine, if you don't want me to teach him, I won't. I'll just let him sit there and do nothing." The specialist's advice sounded to me like, "Give up on Bob; there is no hope for him." But when I stopped pushing Bob to participate in activities, he started to get involved in them on his own. Now we work to introduce new activities and interweave new knowledge and skills into Bob's play in nonthreatening ways.

After reading Vivian Paley's *You Can't Say You Can't Play,* I became more aware of the importance of setting rules for children about including others. Last year I told the fourth- and fifth-grade volunteers in my room that they were not to exclude any of the children in the class. They didn't think they were excluding or rejecting anyone. But when I suggested they include Bob in an activity he wasn't involved in, they admitted they weren't playing with Bob because they didn't like him. I asked them to include Bob anyway, and I reminded them of this from time to time. Within a few months they were including him without being told.

Today I still follow the Individualized Education Plan's goals established for each child, but I am more successful now in helping children achieve these goals. The children in my class learn skills I do not—and could not—teach directly, such as how to get along with one another. Changing to this way of teaching has not been easy. I have had to look at many different issues in my classroom as I struggle with developmentally appropriate practice.

# Mary's mentors reflect . . .

To encourage play, teachers must "set the stage" by offering materials that encourage different types of play. The types of materials are often defined by the philosophy and the goals for the children in the particular setting. How children use these materials, the spaces where they use them, and the conditions of play that adults set can either enhance or constrict the children's experiences. By bringing a variety of materials into the setting, Mary was opening up possibility for play, though she still had much to learn about its nature and functions.

Throughout Mary's account, the power of her existing beliefs and assumptions is evident. We all have such beliefs, and changing them is only possible when they are clear to us and can be considered thoughtfully, as Mary was beginning to do.

The debate over direct instruction and child-initiated activity has been heavily argued among educators. The teacher has to find a balance between too much and too little involvement. We may recognize that children learn best when they are supported in their experiences, and at the same time are able to initiate and direct much of their own activity as they do in play. But choosing whether and how to act in a given situation is still a continuous decisionmaking challenge for the teacher.

Mary has highlighted a key concept in early childhood practice: use of space and arrangement of materials has a profound effect on children's behavior. The division of the environment into functional areas, the materials that are available in each area, and the way the parts are organized into a whole have a major impact on the activities and interactions that occur. Recognizing that design, provisioning, and use of space can either severely curtail or actively enhance opportunities for play and learning, Mary realizes she will continue to be engaged in ongoing questions concerning space and materials.

Mary addresses another problem that causes tension for most teachers. We know that there are skills vitally needed in our society. Reading and writing, various forms of representation and communication, problem solving, math and science skills are important in determining success. Teachers struggle with the issue of covering these topics and teaching the requisite skills. Sometimes this pressure leads teachers to limit children's explorations and interactions so that more time can be devoted to direct instruction. Mary is recognizing that with enough time, thoughtful planning, and supportive teacher interactions, children develop the necessary skills that she thought could be learned only through rote activities, as well as interactive and problem-solving skills that could never have been taught that way.

Once teachers recognize how fundamental play is to children's development, they inevitably face the "continuous struggle" that Mary describes: deciding at each juncture whether to get involved in children's play as well as how to do so. Asking a question, adding a new material or idea to the situation—even joining in the play—all of these are appropriate, effective actions for the teacher to take at certain moments. Yet in other situations, as Mary describes, such actions can be intrusive. Sometimes leaving a child alone and trusting his actions, even when he appears to be doing nothing, is the best course.

Mary is struggling with a problem that many teachers grapple with: inclusion. Is it fair to allow children to exclude others from their play? It is a meaningful question for teachers to ask. Do we protect play experiences and allow children to invite only certain children or do we as adults invite all children to play together? Mary's guidance shows children that inclusion is important. At other times, she may take action to protect an individual's play experience.

Reflect on an activity that you enjoy—a hobby or interest. Think about how quickly time passes when you are involved in this activity, how you feel, how engaged you are. How does this differ from activities that you do because you have to?

Fold a piece of paper in half. On one side make a representation of the barriers to play in your room, and on the other side, represent what play would look like without those barriers. With others write down what you need to get from one side of the paper to the other.

Think about an area or activity (the block area, water table, and so forth) in the classroom. Brainstorm multiple uses for the materials in that area. As you keep this list, think about the way in which you might extend or enhance children's play.

## References and resources for further exploration of this topic

### Books and periodicals

Fromberg, D. 1997. What's new in play research? *Child Care Information Exchange* (November): 53–56.

Fromberg, D. 1998. Play issues in early childhood education. In *Continuing issues in early childhood education,* 2d ed., eds. C. Seefeldt & A. Galper. Columbus, OH: Merrill.

Johnson, J.E., J.F. Christie, & T.D. Yawkey. 1987. *Play and early childhood development.* Glenview, IL: Scott Foresman.

Jones, E., & G. Reynolds. 1992. *The play's the thing: The teacher's role in children's play.* New York: Teachers College Press.

Paley, V.G. 1992. *You can't say you can't play.* Cambridge, MA: Harvard University Press.

Rogers, C., & J. Sawyers. 1988. *Play in the lives of children.* Washington, DC: NAEYC.

Wasserman, S. 1990. *Serious players in the primary classroom: Empowering children through active learning experiences.* New York: Teachers College Press.

### Videotapes

*Child's play: The world of learning.* 1989. 39 min. Beaverton, OR: Educational Productions (800-950-4949).

South Carolina Educational Television. 1987. *A classroom with blocks.* 13 min. Washington, DC: NAEYC.

South Carolina Educational Television. 1993. *Block play: Constructing realities.* 20 min. Washington, DC: NAEYC.

South Carolina Educational Television. 1994. *Sensory play: Constructing realities.* 18 min. Washington, DC: NAEYC.

Stark County, Ohio, School District; North Central Regional Educational Laboratory; Iowa, Nebraska, & Ohio Departments of Education; Jennings Foundation; & NAEYC. 1996. *Play—The seed of learning.* 30 min. The Early Childhood Program: A Place to Grow and Learn series. Washington, DC: NAEYC.

*Time together: Learning to play with young children.* 1990. 30 min. Beaverton, OR: Educational Productions (800-950-4949).

### Websites

The Educational Resources Information Center—http://www.aspenys.com/eric/
Help Children Work with Feelings—http://www.aha4kids.com
I Am Your Child—http://iamyourchild.org
National Association for the Education of Young Children—http://www.naeyc.org
National Child Care Information Center—http://nccic.org
Zero to Three: National Center for Infants, Toddlers, & Families—http://www.zerotothree.org

### Community contacts

Consult your local college or university, child care center, or early childhood educators' networks.

# Guidance

**2**

*Kimberly Boulden, Kay Hiester, and Barbara Walti*

*with Liz Tertell as mentor*

To a great extent, how children learn and develop over time comes from how they are treated, the way they learn to treat others, and the environment in which they function. For this reason classroom management or guidance is at the heart of successful teaching. Here, the meaning of guidance or discipline includes creating a classroom atmosphere that promotes moral development, socialization, and positive self-esteem. Through positive discipline strategies children are treated with respect and dignity, encouraged to develop self-control, and given enhanced opportunities for fully developing as unique individuals.

Guidance is understood only in terms of a system, one in which people are interdependent and each action taken by one person influences the others. What is expected of children, the schedule and routines of the day and week, as well as the techniques employed by adults, all contribute to the system of discipline. To **Kim Boulden** it often seems that some people are born with a natural talent for being able to set appropriate guidelines for children, while others have to work at it, learn by trial and error—and a few hard knocks—and only gradually improve. She says that she looks at those naturally talented people with awe. "Yet when I ask them for words of wisdom," Kim says, "I find that most of the time, if they're honest, they too have struggled in their own way." **Kay Hiester** wrote about guidance because she believes "children's self-esteem is centered around how they were disciplined, the things that do or do not happen to children." Her philosophy is that "these experiences shape the way we feel and the way we handle our feelings in the future." **Barbara Walti** believes that the range of discipline techniques available to redirect behavior often is mystifying to many people who live and work closely with children. "In my generation top-down discipline and corporal punishment were the norm. Now we are exposed to literally dozens of options and hundreds of articles on the subject that oppose the techniques we observed." In her reflective writing Barbara explores her expansions and redefinitions of this important topic.

*—Liz Tertell*

Kimberly Boulden

I began teaching preschool children with special needs five years ago. I have had glorious days when I have driven home feeling satisfied, energized, and knowing there must be a god. On other days my drive home is filled with wondering what all the craziness is about. When the day has been challenging, I have a vulnerable feeling. I contemplate children's behavior and my reactions most humbly then.

The task of helping to mold a young human being into a responsible and good adult is a phenomenal undertaking. I think that anyone who has taken part in this venture has at one point or another questioned how to do it: What should I do in this situation? Is there a win-win response I can find? Am I too authoritarian or too permissive? Well, I don't worry about being too authoritarian, but I feel I'm weak when it comes to being firm and consistent. What are my boundaries, and are they fair? To top it all off, children have an uncanny ability to show you your own strengths and weaknesses. They give you feedback that mirrors yourself, your own issues, your subconscious stuff. Children stretch you to know yourself.

## Learning about myself in relation to teaching

I graduated from college 15 years ago with a degree in elementary education. I had just experienced four years of some rather deep revelations about the nature of the world and myself. I believed I had it all figured out through long philosophical talks with friends, barefoot walks through the campus, a strict vegetarian diet, and an ethical nonconformity to all those "rules" in which people appeared to be stuck. From what I saw as my great awareness, I looked out on the masses of human beings and felt pride about the free spirit I had labored to become. With my teaching degree in hand, I was sure my classroom would be different: children would be allowed to be themselves. They would not be expected to sit quietly in reverence for an all-knowing teacher as I had done during my elementary years in the 1950s. They would feel nurtured, exercise their creativity and their voice, and learn. Ah, the idealism of youth!

*Kimberly Boulden*, M.S., has worked with adults and children with developmental delays. Currently she is a preschool teacher in the Indianapolis area and works with infants and toddlers with special needs.

That summer after graduation I began my work at a child care center as the 3- to 4-year-olds' teacher. Immediately the bubble burst. The experience turned out to be a very panicky, terrifying time of my life. It wasn't the child care center, it was me. My ideas were good; my skill in managing children was not. I have a memory of havoc—the children were running everywhere, and I was trying to bring them together for circle time. I had puppets and other toys to show them — what was the problem? I was devastated and humbled. I remember being most surprised by the anger I felt toward the children. I lasted the summer but did not go back to teaching children for 10 years. Instead, I worked with adults with developmental delays, who were much easier for me. I experienced a successful career, but a lurking fear of failure in the classroom haunted me.

## Looking for a balance

For me a major challenge has been to learn how to provide guidance that is neither too permissive nor too authoritarian. Between the two extremes I search for that delicate balance of moderation. Where this point lies is often a personal interpretation. But I have made gains in my ability to recognize when I've handled a situation fairly and clearly, in a way in which everyone wins. When I began at the child care center, I was definitely on the permissive end of the continuum. I thought I would present the children with a new way. I was missing their need for rules. And as the pendulum swings from one extreme to another, so can a teacher who is unsure of herself. A permissive moment can create other moments that are punitive and angry.

I am reminded of the story of three families going on vacation to South Carolina. The children in all three families didn't want to go to South Carolina; they wanted to go to Disney World. One couple who parented in a permissive fashion told their pleading children, "Oh, we're sorry. We didn't realize how important it was for you to go to Disney World." They called the airline, changed their reservations, and went to Orlando. The authoritarian parents told their children, "Who do you think you are to tell us what to do? We're going to South Carolina whether you like it or not! Go pack your bags." The third couple told their children, "We're glad you let us know your vacation wish. Disney World is a good idea for a family sometime. Let's plan that another year [and they meant it]. But this year we're going to South Carolina, so go pack your bags." These parents were using the authoritative style, which has been proven most effective.

## Back to my beginnings

In my own home as a child I was confronted with permissive, authoritarian, and authoritative styles of parenting. This pattern is not at all uncommon and can create tension in a family and confusion in a child. I believe many people who are involved with children flip back and forth between these modes at one time or another, especially when they are emotionally stressed.

In teaching I have found that children evoke the deep layers of myself, layers of my earliest fears. Some of my fears go back to the boundary issues of the permissive/authoritative/authoritarian topologies. As a teacher I have experienced what many parents and teachers have — that children continually push and stretch us. We find ourselves flipping around in each parenting mode, and our particular histories and weaknesses surface.

For me this goes back to having been a "nice girl" and not wanting to hurt people's feelings. Figuring out how to handle children's behavior continues to call on me to go back, and back, and back — and deeper within myself.

## Reexamining teaching habits and classroom rules

In beginning my new career of teaching preschool children with special needs, I worked in a school that provided excellent training. My belief that interactive learning environments are effective with children with or without special needs was reinforced through the training. This educational approach is what I have found keeps children engaged and active. For me that's key. When children are doing something that has little meaning to them, behavior problems erupt. They have far less need to act out or disrupt others when they are challenged and supported.

I was making progress in my guidance techniques, but I relied heavily on time-out. I moved to the public school system later and for two years continued to use time-out. I look back on the times when I sat a child down in a chair, specifically placed in the room for the purpose of discipline, and now I can't believe it.

In one of my classes, we read Vivian's Paley's *You Can't Say You Can't Play*. As an aside, she said it would have been good to ditch the time-out chair years ago (not her words exactly). I was startled by her statement since time-out was a common practice for me. When the class next met, other people also voiced surprise at Paley's view. Paley

had come to see the time-out chair as the teacher's version of exclusion, of saying, "You can't play."

As I read further in Paley's book, I began to think about the rules in my classroom. Were they for children's safety or was I making a value judgment about what I believe? Were all my rules consistent with the expectations I had for children, or did some impede play and growth, as time-out may do?

I spent some time revisiting the rules in my classroom, both the written ones and those that seemed to be in operation although they hadn't been explicitly expressed. I thought about them and what they were saying to my children. I looked at changing them. For example, my rule about not building blocks higher than children's shoulders had a rationale: I don't want a child to get hit on the head. A real safety issue, but what about all the learning and excitement of building taller structures? This was a problem until it occurred to me that I could meet both concerns. Now when children wish to build taller structures, everyone in the block area must wear a hard hat! Not all questions about rules are as easy to resolve, but I have begun to think more creatively about classroom rules.

Sam has been in my class for two years. In the past when Sam was expected to share, he had a temper tantrum. Last year, whenever he was on the verge of a tantrum, I placed him in the time-out chair. This step never helped and only increased his anger and mine. This year I have used a much more effective strategy. When Sam wants to play with a toy that lends itself to turn taking or sharing, I make clear that he must decide whether he can take turns with others or find something else to do. At first he fell on the floor in tears and temper. But when I paid no attention, he eventually stopped and joined us. This was a big breakthrough for Sam and for me.

I have learned not to exclude a child by sending her to a time-out area, which labels the child "bad," but rather to redirect her to another activity, area, or interest. The child is always welcome to return when she thinks she can participate appropriately. The child is more likely to develop self-control when she is given the choice about when to return rather than the clock or timer being the deciding factor. I have also learned that children often need help or support to reenter an activity. I can be the support that individual children need to return with ease.

The time-out chair is forever retired in my classroom, and all the children feel more safe, even those children who were never in it. I know this because a parent told me that the thing her son likes most about his new school is that no one sits on the time-out chair. She said it used to terrify him when other children were left there at his previous school. Although he himself never experienced time-out, it caused him great anguish when others did.

In my classroom at this particular level of my self-evaluation, I would say I'm still learning to consistently practice authoritative — not authoritarian or permissive — teaching. Sometimes I flip back to one of the extremes quite by surprise to myself. I'm told these flips are not usually apparent to others, but inside myself I feel it happening.

When one girl from another classroom hangs on me and begs to come to my room, I usually give in, not wanting to hurt her feelings. And at other times I lose my patience and angrily tell the children *not* to go into the gym storage closet but to sit quietly. Managing a group is an ongoing challenge.

## Who am I in this classroom?

I can recognize when we as a class are together and harmonious, and much of that depends on me. I believe that, as teachers, we are the creators of the climate and we can shape the atmosphere. The teacher sets the tone, though some days she may not feel this is true.

I am grateful for having a fresh start each year — for that matter, each day. Teachers can change their minds, but when it's a however-the-wind-blows kind of change, children feel confused and rebel. I had confused children one day when I changed my mind too many times about whether we would get out the trampoline. They became cranky.

When in anger I demand certain behaviors of the children, it doesn't work long for me either; neither does being too "nice" or lacking any rules. I consider myself a gentle spirit, and I have had to learn to find the right balance.

This is the way a good day might go. As the children arrive in the morning, I'm very happy to see them. I greet each child individually and let them all know they may play for a few minutes before we go to the gym. This is our routine. When it's time to go, I tell the children in a friendly way to come to the door. After a few moments and a reminder, if any child is still playing, I look that child straight in the eye and with a clear intention — as though I'm not expecting any trouble and know without a doubt that the child will join us — repeat the request. When I am speaking from this "mental place," I rarely have any management problems. Although it's hard to describe, I know when I've got it — not being mad or suppressive, just dead sure that we're *all* going to the gym.

I ask for this participation daily. I could change this at any time and make going to the gym a personal choice, but for now I'm satisfied with my decision. It has taken me a while to accept this role — that I decide what goes on in the classroom — not from a position of control but from one of leadership. Though exceptions to a given routine or plan can occur, it's my responsibility to be aware of how things are going, think of possible options, and carefully weigh each decision.

When my attitude and approach suggest clearly that I have no expectation of trouble, the children usually do very well. They seem to feel safe: they know what to do, and they know other kids won't hurt them (because the teacher is aware of what is going on in the room). I believe that this understanding results from warm, nurturing relationships that develop over time between children and adults and the knowledge that children cooperate with those who honor and enjoy them.

### Still learning

I have learned that children are more likely to follow a rule when I remind them of it in advance; for example, "Remember to ride your tricycle *slowly* to the playground." I am learning to be present consistently when help is needed between children. Often this means guiding the children, to a greater or lesser degree, in solving their own disputes. Sometimes young children can't figure out solutions entirely on their own; they need models of what to say or do.

One way I help is by encouraging children to tell each other in specific terms what they want. For example, if two children are quarreling in the sandbox, I encourage each to say what it is that he or she would like the other to do. Instead of just saying, "I don't like it when you take my toy," a child can add, "I want you to ask first."

And what about those times when I drive home wondering what all the craziness that day was about? I can assure you that days or moments like this still occur. Experienced teachers confirm that those moments happen to everyone, which gives me some comfort. Every teacher I know — and every parent — admits to having such experiences. I know that at times I get emotionally stressed and don't handle situations well. Even when I'm in a good mood, I don't always handle situations well. Not always doing the best thing is part of teaching. But I find that as I take time to reflect on my experiences — negative and positive — I improve.

## Looking at children in a new way

As I continue to learn from colleagues and look at who I am, I find that I am beginning to look at children in new ways. Last year I had trouble liking a child in my class. Remembering a wise teacher's words to me — that the first step with a challenging child is to like him — I began thinking about this child at night. With a bit of distance, I could see that he might be giving me and the other children a hard time because he had a sensitive ego and was eager for attention. Lacking positive social skills, he got attention by annoying others, especially when his ego was bruised.

I thought more about this child and began looking at him differently. I no longer saw his behavior in simple black-and-white terms. I began to see many shades of gray. I went to school the next day with a fresh attitude. Before my eyes the child seemed transformed, not in his ability to get along with other children but in my image of him. As the year went on, he made a lot of progress. I've had other experiences like this and found that peace with a situation begins first with peace within myself. Now, if a child is having behavior problems in my class, I think first how I view the child, how I categorize him. I find that changing my expectations creates a way for children to break out of the mold I've cast.

One revelation I have had in my teaching career is that ideas I hold as truth may not be so at all. The time-out chair is an example. As teachers we can reflect on each child and educate ourselves about best practice in guiding young children. We have many decisions to make, moment to moment, and we need to remain open to change.

# Kimberly's mentor reflects . . .

By learning to set limits, follow through, and create an appropriate environment for positive guidance and discipline, Kim helps children develop self-control and prosocial skills. Critical to this process is her movement toward an authoritative style of teaching and use of reasoning. Giving children the whys behind rules or behavioral limits encourages them to construct an understanding of the reasons for exerting self-control. Kim describes the process of constructing her own whys for the limits she decides are important.

The authoritative approach involves setting high expectations for each child's behavior and providing responsive support to help the child reach these. This can happen only when the teacher sees each child as an individual. Kim determines expectations and provides the support appropriate to each child's unique capabilities and needs. As Kim and I discussed, the lens through which we view a child is clouded by our own experiences, including the expectations of adults who influenced our development. Other teachers' opinions about the child or the child's behaviors that remind us of things we don't like about ourselves further cloud or distort the lens. We make assumptions about why the child acts as he does, and we begin responding to the child in certain ways—often reinforcing undesired behaviors.

Sometimes we need to clean our lens or way of viewing a child. We must take time to think about our expectations and the images and roles we are casting the child in. Only when we are able to view each child as having the capability to be strong, powerful, and successful will we allow her to confront her problems and increase her self-control.

As Kim describes, the teacher draws on stated and unstated goals and beliefs to create rules and classroom guidance. She comes to see the need to examine and clarify her rules and methods to make sure that they support classroom goals. For example, in a constructivist classroom that strives to encourage autonomy, teacher guidance is geared to enable children to get their own materials and solve their own problems instead of

getting solutions from the adults. In such classrooms children can participate with adults in developing rules.

In Kim's classroom encouraging and respecting children's play is a
priority. Keeping this goal clearly in mind, she rethinks her limits for children's block building. In the end she finds a way to support play *and*
provide a safe environment.

As she looks at her classroom, Kim recognizes how essential clear,
consistent rules and systematic follow-through are to maintaining effective
classroom management. Her authoritative leadership conveys her own self-
control and respect for the children, while it clearly communicates expectations for their behavior. When children know what to expect and understand class rules, they feel secure and develop trust.

Think about your own childhood and how you were disciplined. What did you learn from these experiences? Are there
discipline techniques you use in your classroom that go back to
your childhood? List the techniques you find useful and those
you would like to change.

Make a list of rules—both written and implied—that you apply in
your classroom. Consider each rule. Do the rules reflect your
philosophy and goals? In what ways might you go about adapt-
ing a rule?

Choose one discipline technique that you would like to change.
List all the alternate techniques that you might try.

Make a drawing, sculpture, or other representation of your
personal philosophy of discipline. Depict how other influences
in your life—family, workshops, education, and so on—have
affected your philosophy.

P unishment and discipline — are they the same? I used to think so. Today the two words are seen as meaning two different things. *Punishment* has a very negative meaning and conjures up images of embarrassment, shame, or pain for the child. *Discipline* does not have such a negative connotation but still implies use of corrective measures when a child behaves in an unacceptable way.

In the past few years, I have added a third word to my behavior management vocabulary — *redirecting*. This word seems much gentler than either punishment or discipline. For me, redirecting has been the answer to a lot of behavioral problems I have encountered with pre-school children.

## My history with discipline

I was raised in a large, easy-going family, and I have no recollection of harsh or physical punishments in our household. But school was another matter. Since I was the oldest child, my starting school was a new, exciting experience for the family. Mom made all my dresses, and I got new underwear and socks from Sears. I even got to pick out my new shoes. Did I ever feel special on that first day! As I waited for the school bus, I suddenly felt overwhelmed. Mom and the bus driver had to coax me onto the bus, and as we pulled away, leaving Mom behind, tears welled up in my eyes.

When we reached the school, we waited for our names to be called to find out which class we were in. When my name was called, I timidly got in line. My teacher was a very, very, very tall lady (or so it seemed to my 6-year-old eyes). After everyone was in line, we marched into the school. I had never seen the inside of the school before. I was so busy looking around that I bumped into the child ahead of me. "Pay attention, little girl," said my teacher in a stern voice. Everything was so new to me; I thought I *was* paying attention!

Entering the classroom, we were directed to our seats and told to sit quietly as the teacher looked through her paperwork. I can recall the excitement and the smell of new crayons, yellow paper tablets, and

**Kay Hiester,** A.A., has taught nurturing parenting classes in her community and serves on several child care boards. She runs her own accredited family child care program, which she has operated for 29 years.

paste. Eager to see what was in my desk, I quietly lifted the lid a crack to peek inside, and wham! I let the lid drop as the teacher's ruler smacked hard across my knuckles. I had just received the first physical discipline I had ever experienced, and it was in front of 30 peers. Embarrassed, mortified, hurt, and scared, I was immediately in tears. The experience was devastating.

The episode on this first day of school has stayed with me and will always. As I teach today, I think about my expectations of children. I think about their feelings: what happened before they arrived that morning? How do they feel as they experience new activities and materials? I think about these children, who each is and what discipline techniques may be used in the child's home.

## A partnership with each family

Parents naturally have their own beliefs and ideas on how a child should be raised. These family philosophies and practices frequently show up in the interactions and behaviors of the children.

One girl apparently is disciplined with the "bad, bad girl" method. When Cary spilled his juice, she immediately stood up, shook her finger in his face, and yelled, "Bad, bad girl Cary." When I knocked a full gallon of milk off the counter, I got the same "bad, bad girl" treatment. Another child is always asking me, "Are you going to beat my butt?" And when one of us asks Sonja to do something, no matter what it is, she starts counting to three.

All of us grow up in families with cultural and individual approaches to desired and undesired behavior. I regard it as my job to understand the techniques each family in the program uses to discipline their children. I find out about what parents want for their child and what they believe in. I talk about my own goals, beliefs, and methods. We do not always agree on our practices, but we agree to work together, listen to each other, and work toward what is best for their child. Accomplishing this partnership is not easy by any means, but I have no choice but to take into account the beliefs, priorities, and concerns of families I work with.

I go about creating this open communication in several ways. Before a child enrolls, the family and I discuss the center's philosophy and practices. We talk as often as possible, sometimes daily. We have formal conferences and many informal conversations. I always listen to what parents want from this program and take their concerns seriously.

One time a parent came to me and said that I was not strict enough in reprimanding her child. We spent a great deal of time talking about what was happening at my center and at the child's home. It boiled down to this: she was worried about her child's success in school — a very real concern for parents. Instead of just trying to change the parent's mind about punishment style, I found out what her fears and hopes were. Had I simply informed her of other techniques and not discovered her concerns, we never would have worked together.

## Rethinking time-out

Some years ago I became aware of the technique known as time-out, and I decided to try it with the children in my own setting. I designated a certain secluded part of the room to use as the time-out area. I planned to use time-out whenever a child was misbehaving or out of control — the magic answer to all the behavior problems in my program! Everywhere I looked, time-out was being praised: in professional journals, women's magazines, and the news media. Articles discussed the marvels of how well this worked for everyone; it was to be the cure for all arguments, disputes, and behavioral problems in children of all ages.

I introduced this marvel to the children during morning circle time. We talked about why we might need a time-out and where time-out was located. The children even did some role playing about how to go to this area if they were instructed to do so.

Almost immediately a disagreement arose over whose turn it was to play with the Etch-a-Sketch. I tried having the two children involved in the dispute resolve the conflict in a mutual way, after which one hauled off and decked the other. He was sent to time-out and went willingly — almost as if it were a reward! After all, he got to go to this special area before anyone else.

As time went on and I tried to use time-out effectively, it did not seem to work as I had thought. Yes, it separated one child from the others, thus stopping the conflict. But something just did not feel right about it.

The more I pondered the rationale for time-out, the more doubtful I became about what I was doing. Suddenly it dawned on me that I was using the tool as punishment! I was not using time-out to teach children to solve their own problems; I was not helping them develop self-control. Instead I was using time-out to punish inappropriate behavior. I have changed my way of thinking and now rarely use time-out in my program. If it is used, it serves as a self-quieting time and not as a punishment for the child. A child sometimes needs to be alone and regain control of her behavior. When this is the case, the child uses the opportunity to go off by herself and spends time alone. A child usually chooses to take along a book or pencil and paper with which to occupy herself until she is ready to rejoin the other children. Sometimes a child wants a time-out and asks if she may go.

As a self-quieting time, time-out works well. With this approach, the child learns to recognize when he needs quieting time alone; however, it does take time and patience to get children to the point of knowing when they are in need of this alone time. The benefits for children are that it calms them and helps them regain control of their actions.

One boy in my group is extremely moody and at times cannot seem to function well with the other children. I have found that removing him from the rest of the children helps him deal with his moods. From the start I took pains to let him know that he was not being punished. Given a choice of activities to take with him to time-out, he rarely picks anything but the zoo animals — for him they seem to work magic. He plays for a long time by himself in this area and is very engaged. Once or twice a week he asks to go into his "special place." His requests seem to occur when he is having a difficult day, something he now recognizes and knows how to deal with on his own. I see this as real progress. His moods are less frequent as he seems to be getting a handle on his own behaviors. Each time, when he is ready, he comes back and rejoins the other children as if he had been there all along, but now he is in control of his actions.

I know I must remember that not every technique works with every child, and sometimes we must try a number of things before we find one that works well with a particular child. When we do find something that is effective, we count it as a huge success — for us and the child involved.

## Taking on tattling

"Kay, Henry's running in the house."

"Kay, Mary's using too much soap."

"Kay, Ty won't share."

"Kay, Ali isn't taking turns on the slide."

"Kay, Carol didn't ask if she could get the trucks out."

"Kay, Bruce was going to jump on the chair."

One thing that nearly drives me crazy is tattling! I think it's the one behavior that annoys me more than any other. Some children just seem to have a tattling personality. I have tried all sorts of ways to break them of the habit — from my stop-in-your-tracks stare to exclaiming, "Stop tattling." Nothing seemed to work.

I know, of course, that sometimes coming to an adult is appropriate, such as when another child's actions could result in injury. During circle time the children and I have discussed at length when they should report to me about what someone else has done. We brainstormed various situations. Some of the children's examples included when a toddler is opening the door and might slip outside unnoticed by me; when someone is choking; when someone is getting into the medicines; and when a child starts climbing over the fence. From these illustrations I felt that the children had a good grasp of the kinds of actions that warrant reporting. Still, the gray areas of when to tell and when not to are hard for children to understand.

Lately I have decided to use another tactic: ignoring. When a child runs to me to tattle, I simply do not hear the news. I immediately turn my attention away from that child. After several days of this new strategy, tattling sharply diminished. Even my hard-core tattlers caught on and changed their behavior.

## Facing our monsters

A few weeks ago a monster cropped up in our group — biting! Whenever this happens it causes havoc among the children and even more among the parents. Every year we've had a problem with at least one child biting, and it has always driven me crazy. When a child bit another, I invariably reacted very strongly. Biting seemed to me the worst thing a child could do, and I could not understand why a child wanted to bite anyone. Besides, biting always brought out my concerns about making sure that the children in my care are safe, as well as learning to abide by our society's rules and get along with each other. This year I decided I needed to take a more thoughtful look at the children's biting behavior. I started to observe closely.

I saw that children often bite in anger. At other times they bite in retaliation or just out of frustration. Through this observation and through reading about the problem and children's stages of development, I learned more about what triggers biting. Lacking the words and sometimes the self-control to express their feelings another way, some young children bite.

I am making a point of communicating with *all* the children about anger: that it is okay to be angry and that we must find appropriate ways to show our anger. And when I myself am angry, I talk to the children about it to model this way of dealing with one's strong feelings.

I also communicate with other staff. When we have a child who bites, we keep close watch on her. All of us look for the signals children give when they are upset, the warning signs that might precede biting. We work hard to redirect children's frustrations and help them find appropriate ways to solve their problems or express their emotions.

As I learn more about biting and examine my own fears, the monster is fading. Biting, of course, isn't gone forever. But with a new way to look at it, I address this behavior head-on instead of waiting for it to sneak up on me. I have a stronger understanding of the problem and some strategies for prevention and intervention.

With children we all deal with issues of control on a daily basis. Food power struggles and cleanup time are two more issues I have grappled with. At one time I was obsessed with what and how much children ate. After all, children need a good, balanced diet, right? I saw my job as the food warden policing the kinds of food and amounts that each child ate. After countless battles, I have slowly changed my expectations and my tactics. I am still committed to good nutrition, but now children are involved in the management process. They take an active role in helping to choose our menus and prepare our meals.

Likewise, I have done some thinking about cleanup. After looking at my expectations of the children and what I wanted to accomplish, I

changed my approach. I still have
trouble at times, but I realize that learning
to cooperate takes time. Now I see cleanup as a
valid learning activity. Sometimes children choose what
they will clean up. At other times, the group fills a container,
and together children count the toys. Or each child picks a number
or color and then puts away objects of that number or color. I see
children's cooperation and decisionmaking skills developing.

In organizing our classroom I have involved the children in deciding how and where we should store everything. This involvement
seems to reduce struggles, and I no longer police the children. I
continue to think abut my expectations for both the group and the
children as individuals, but my expectations are based more strongly
on appropriate developmental levels.

## Moving toward new views

A few years ago I enrolled in a class called Redirecting Children's
Behavior. The instructor became an invaluable support, helping me
with behavior problems I have encountered in my child care home. I
learned that children act out because of four basic reasons: avoidance,
attention, revenge, and power. I learned to identify children's
behavior in terms of reasons and then deal with behaviors in a way
that fits the source.

Now that I am more in touch with why children act as they do in
my program, I also have changed my way of dealing with undesired
behaviors from the old punishment methods to time-outs and now to
redirection. Looking at behaviors in a new light, I don't simply con-
clude that the child is being bad. I also look more closely at myself,
recognizing how important a role I play — not principally in terms of
controlling behavior, but in terms of anticipating and gently guiding it.

What I have learned has been invaluable to me not only in working
with children but in relating to adults. Writing this journal has caused
me to realize how I have changed my ways of thinking and acting.

I know I must continue to think about who I am in the lives of the
children. Before I can do that, I must know the person I am and where
I come from. I also know that education and professional development are never wasted, and I will always continue to stay abreast of
any new ideas, understandings, and methods in my work with children. I will continue to think about the many issues that arise in
discipline and redirection. More and more I recognize that young
children's emotions and behaviors and the way I deal with them are
central in children's development.

# Kay's mentor reflects ...

Kay talks about the cultural values and norms that play a role in the guidance each family provides. We now understand that learning more about each family's beliefs and expectations is important in providing effective discipline outside the home. Kay has recognized that talking with families about expectations, behavior, and management techniques enables professionals to support the values of each family at the same time they maintain their own. Teaching and discipline practices may have to be negotiated, but this process can only begin when there is shared understanding. Kay created an environment that encourages dialogue between families and her center.

She also explores her own values in respect to "button pushing" and "pet peeves." The relationships between teachers and children often test the limits of each adult's acceptance and capabilities. We all seem to have one or more pet peeves that test our patience. While someone else might not feel the way Kay does about tattling, that teacher may find some other commonplace behavior unacceptable. The children in Kay's care come to know that she does not like tattling. This is part of what they are learning about interacting with others outside of their own family. For adults the first step in learning to deal with our own special issues is acknowledging the behaviors that we can't tolerate. When we function as team members, it is particularly important to work out the ways in which pet peeves will be handled.

Adults have their own myths and misconceptions, passed down through families, about how to handle children's behaviors. For example, some people have a ready response to biting: "Bite the child back." In toilet training, feeding, and any area of children's behavior and development, there are strongly held beliefs that can interfere with solving a problem. Kay sees that to deal with these myths we must learn more about children. She does this in many ways—by reading, talking to others, observing the children in her care, and reflecting carefully on her own beliefs. She acknowledges her apprehensions surrounding the issue of biting and explores other options than time-out as a consequence for behaviors. This process of addressing her biases and gaining new information gives her well-grounded new strategies and approaches to old problems.

Through such efforts Kay builds the essential links between guiding children toward self-control and supporting children's ability to understand and manage their own emotions. Whether she is reflecting on the issue of biting, tattling, or cleanup, children's feelings come up. In each case Kay describes a process of dialogue, which both encourages children to recognize their feelings and enables them to gain increasing skills and options for responding to them. This process makes a vital contribution to each child's developing self-control.

Think about a time period when you felt you had little control over events. What did you experience? How did you interact with others? If you assumed some control or felt that your opinions were heard, did this change your feelings or your behavior?

Make a timeline of your teaching practices. Start with the discipline techniques you employed at the beginning of your teaching career. Make note of when you began working on other strategies. Think about what encouraged these changes.

With colleagues, make a list or a representation of behaviors that "push your buttons" and describe how you feel in such situations. Take some time to think about the ways you support each other. Make a plan for handling these pet-peeve issues in the classroom.

Barbara Walti

O n a Friday evening my phone rings, and the caller is one of the moms I visit each month in my role as a parent educator in our school district's Parents As First Teachers program. Sounding stressed, she tells me that her 3-year-old is now testing her authority at bedtime and has throughout the day. She asks about using the time-out chair. "Let's consider some other options," I suggest and propose redesigning portions of the day to give her son more opportunities to make decisions and choices. We start thinking together of strategies.

## Discipline

A number of years ago, I accepted a fourth-grade teaching position while my husband was attending graduate school. I had 32 children in my class, 20 boys and 12 girls. The school, in the middle of a corn-field in southwestern Ohio, went from 7:45 A.M. to 3:20 P.M. The students had gym and music twice a week and art twice a year! No recess! Looking back, I wonder how the children survived the day. What did they do with all the normal energy of childhood? They did what Mallory did — they found alternative ways to release their energy. Mallory and another boy invented a contest to see who could touch a wall clock, which stuck out from the wall at a 90-degree angle where the children waited in the lunch line. Mallory could touch it with a great vertical jump; but his touch was too hard, and the clock came crashing to the ground.

I was called to the scene of the "crime," and I dutifully marched Mallory to the principal's office. His punishment: three whacks with the principal's paddle and custodial duty until the value of the clock was repaid. I confess that at the time I did not deem the corporal punishment as excessive. Repaying the value of the clock still seems justified as I recall the incident today. However, I cringe at the thought of an innocent childhood incident being treated with insensitive adult authority.

*Barbara Walti, M.S., has been an early childhood teacher in both private and public schools, a parent educator, and director of a preschool program in an elementary school. Currently she teaches early childhood special education in the Indianapolis Public Schools.*

*Gradually she helped the children realize
that they were personally in charge
of their behavior: each was
his own boss.*

I had not thought of that incident until today. This approach to discipline would not be considered an option now. What did Mallory learn from his punishment? How many other times did he meet with corporal punishment and question his self-worth? If Mallory had had the opportunity to explore a logical consequence of his action, the incident would have been a learning experience rather than a punitive one.

## Learning to trust children

When my youngest child started first grade, I was ready to return to the profession I loved — teaching. I had the privilege of teaching at a well-respected nursery school. The program became one of the first sites in Indiana to be accredited by the National Association for the Education of Young Children. I learned the concepts of developmentally appropriate practice, the curriculum approach of High/Scope, and the importance of motor development in young children. We team taught, with each member of the team having equal responsibilities.

While teaching at this nursery school, I began to expand my repertoire of discipline methods. Looking back on those years and rethinking the topic of discipline, I think about an experienced teacher who taught me so much about discipline. Her understanding of the needs, rights, and responsibilities of children was impressive. She was an outspoken champion for the concept that children could determine for themselves, in most instances, the amount of time they needed to rethink behaviors or get emotions under control. At that point in my career, I had a very hard time with this concept. I felt much more comfortable with the notion that I, the experienced adult, could determine what was best for the child. Being in charge was part of the job of being a teacher. Although I did not perceive myself as a top-down behavior manager, I now recognize that I disciplined children that way.

My colleague's foundation for discipline rested with a simple idea: *trust.* She believed that trust is the most important component of any relationship, whether that trust exists between parent and child or teacher and student. She also believed that trust is not innate in people. At birth the child does not yet trust but has that need and capacity. Trust is acquired through the many instances, large and small, in which needs are met and promises are kept.

A teacher-friend remembers asking the children each fall who they thought the boss was in the classroom. They all eagerly said that the teacher was the boss. She would talk with them about the teacher's role, which included setting up the environment, getting supplies, planning activities. Gradually she helped the children realize that they were personally in charge of their behavior: each was his own boss.

Building trust takes time, consistent routines, fair rules, and respectful interactions. Children who experience these feel safe and can trust and be trusted. My friend's behavior-management philosophy reminds me of the saying: if you don't let children down, they won't let you down.

My colleague spoke with conviction about trust as the cornerstone of behavior management in the classroom and at home. Her confidence reminds me of the beautiful NAEYC poster: *Trust children to succeed.* How simple!

During the six years that I taught in a regular preschool program, I had few serious discipline problems. That situation now seems to me a very sheltered one. No child had attention deficit hyperactivity disorder or other special needs. Every child was parented by a mother and father who lived together in what appeared to be a stable home environment. I just accepted this as the norm, but, with what I've seen over the last three years those children now seem to have existed in utopia.

Of course, with any group of children there are behavior-management issues. When I used reflective listening, *I*-messages, encouragement, and natural and logical consequences, these behaviors usually improved. Our center's teachers subscribed to the practice of "catching children being good," which encouraged positive role models and nurtured self-esteem. We tried to ignore misbehavior whenever possible. These techniques usually worked well with our population of typically developing preschoolers from good home situations. These children lived in a trusting world, surrounded by people they could trust and rely upon daily.

## Facing tougher problems

In a later career shift, I became the director of the extended-day program for kindergartners in a suburban neighborhood community. Some of the children were living in homes with great stresses, including divorce, abuse, neglect, and self-destructive behaviors. I began to encounter discipline issues of a different magnitude from that I had previously experienced.

I had been at my new position for only six weeks when Timmy arrived. It was apparent that his emotional stability was fragile. He had recently moved with his mother from another state after his parents divorced. He was violent toward the other children and the teachers. His mother reported that he had seen aggression at home, but his behaviors had surfaced only since his enrollment in my program. Later I discovered that he had attended another program before

coming to ours and had been removed because his behavior and language were disruptive.

Timmy was able to verbalize how he felt: that separating from Dad was unsettling. He would cry out before the mirror in the bathroom, "I never got to say good-bye to him." Timmy's ability to talk about his anxiety helped us to understand his concerns and support him in coping with his fears. He was angry, scared, and aggressive. Because his aggressive behaviors were unpredictable, our classroom was like an outburst waiting to happen.

My usual behavior-management techniques proved inadequate and ineffective with Timmy. The teachers and I encouraged Timmy to talk about his feelings and made sure we were available to him. We gave Timmy opportunities to release his energy without aggression through physical activities — obstacle courses, trike riding, tumbling, and the like. We also offered calming activities, such as water play, clay molding, and reading or playing a quiet game with an adult.

But eventually when we discussed the results of the evaluation process, our team concluded that our program was not able to provide Timmy and his family with the therapeutic support they needed. We worked to refer them to an agency that could provide more intensive services.

Having no previous experiences in dealing with children suffering from emotional trauma, I chose to work closely with the principal and the school support team. I spoke often with Timmy's mother. I saw that my usual techniques would accomplish little without an improvement in the whole family's well-being. Timmy needed support, but it was his family that could do the most for him. I talked with Timmy's mom about counseling and evaluation. Timmy and his mother together went twice to the counselor, and because of her own difficulties she continued in counseling on her own.

I was beginning to learn that teaching and supporting young children also means supporting their families. Often what that means is being there for families when they call for assistance or need information about resources in the community. I find that having conversations with parents both in and out of the classroom helps build our partnership.

Another important lesson I've learned is how beneficial it is for parents to participate in the classroom. When a parent is with us, I can teach and model behavior-management techniques, and the parent can see that these methods work. Family members can ask questions and develop or adapt techniques to fit their individual style and personality. Sometimes as the situation arises, I offer a way of looking at the child's behavior. Parents also can teach me about the approaches that work at home. From parents I learn not only about their individual strengths as parents but also about their children's strengths and needs. I can learn about the individual family's culture, beliefs, and values. Knowing a family is key to building a strong partnership.

## In over my head?

My mind fast-forwards to the next school year and the tough challenges it brought. In my class were two children who had suicidal thoughts and made plans to carry them out. Another child had characteristics of fetal alcohol syndrome. I felt totally overwhelmed by their aggressive behaviors and the depression they were experiencing. I felt totally untrained to identify their symptoms and understand their behaviors and even more uncertain of how to communicate with and manage these children.

I was very lucky to have the support of a marvelous principal and a school psychologist, who took the time to help me understand why these behaviors were happening in my classroom and how I could best respond and respect each child's characteristics. Initially I believed that our environment must be organized wrongly; otherwise these children would not become disruptive and destructive. The school psychologist helped me understand that, in fact, the opposite was true. Because our environment was nurturing, supportive, and inclusive, these children felt safe to act out their frustrations, knowing that caring adults would support them. This made me feel better. Problem behaviors or not, we were meeting important emotional needs, at least to a degree.

One day 5-year-old Brett approached me with one of his shoestrings hanging around his neck. "I'm going to threaten myself," he said and then told me his plan of climbing a tree and tying the string to a branch and jumping to his death. I listened in horror. I gently removed the shoestring from his neck, resolving to talk with his mom as soon as possible.

Brett's mother worked in our program, and over the last two years we had established a strong professional relationship. Witnessing Brett's classroom behavior, she revealed her concern that it resulted from the family dysfunction he was experiencing. Seeking out counseling for herself and her children, she was able to get help from trained professionals and to see that her children got it too. Brett grew stronger emotionally and so did she. Feeling empowered to remove herself from an abusive marital relationship, she reported that for the first time her children felt secure in their home. That year was a long, emotionally draining year for her and for me as we wove together our professional and personal roles in working for Brett's benefit.

In the classroom we worked on substituting language for unacceptable behaviors, encouraging Brett to talk about his feelings instead of acting them out. With help Brett developed strategies to cope with his feelings, such as "talking to his body" to relax on his own. We gave reassurance to Brett by making sure he sensed our presence and making eye contact with him. We guaranteed him a little time alone when he needed it — not time-out, just a chance to be away from the group and by himself. Now a year later Brett is successfully completing his second year of kindergarten. Through supportive adults he is rebuilding himself emotionally, which has positive effects on his learning and on all areas of his development.

## Getting help from others

The school psychologist is a person I rely on and talk with as I try to understand how to best serve these children and use effective behavior-management techniques, which may go well beyond those that work with emotionally stable children. The usual early childhood guidance methods, such as natural and logical consequences, reflective listening, and redirection, are insufficient for children with weak self-regulatory behaviors and other emotional stressors.

Some of these children, I saw, did not feel safe; they were frightened and sad. They also were angry. Perhaps by behaving in negative ways they were seeking attention, limits, some type of structure in their lives. By understanding that these emotionally fragile children were out of control and seeking limits from supportive adults, I gained a new way of working with them, of talking with them. For example, saying, "I will not let you hurt me and I will not let you hurt yourself" and "If you can't get your behavior under control, then I will help you" enabled me to create a dialogue with the children. The dialogue itself added structure and limits, creating safety and security.

I learned that some children with emotional difficulties need extra structure in the classroom. When they get it, their negative behaviors decrease. With the school psychologist's input, I became more aware of the children's needs and what I could do to help. In other situations in this and other settings, I have benefited from collaboration and consultation with various specialists.

During the last three years, I have encountered numerous children whose personal stories include trauma, and I believe it is played out in the classroom. I can only imagine the uncertainties that they face each day in their young lives. I cannot imagine the extent to which some of these young spirits have endured emotional and physical pain every day of their lives.

Recently I encountered a new term that has helped me understand some of the psychological processes affecting all children with respect to setting limits. Many parents can be said to enfold their children in an "empathic envelope" of compassion, consistent consequences, and communication. But some children have not experienced this enveloping security that consistency and appropriate limits provide. Early childhood teachers are often the first to notice emotional, social, or academic differences in children, and we are often the first to communicate these concerns to parents. It is a big responsibility.

The children I have described challenged me to discover alternative methods of behavior management for enabling children to remain in the safe, secure, predictable environment called school. For many children the school or early childhood program is the most consistent, protected place they know. I realize I must keep looking for ideas, support, and encouragement to become receptive to all children in my program and to serve them well. I want to enlarge my circle of professional resources and become more aware of resources for children and their families. Now I seek a circle of support for myself.

Recognizing that children communicate their needs and fears through their behaviors, I know how important observation is. I find that by observing more closely and recording anecdotal notes, I have been able to predict behavior patterns and take action to reduce problems. For example, I might rearrange the environment, remove some equipment, or intervene more directly in peer exchanges.

## Building support systems

Critically examining our own expectations of the children in our classrooms and the design of our physical environment can help us create an optimum environment in which all children can feel included and can succeed. Every child needs support systems. The professional must use a variety of supports to build a strong structure for the physical and emotional environment of the classroom. These supports may include older students, participating parents, or foster grandparents and other senior-citizen volunteers who listen to children's stories, provide positive role models, and assist children who need to release their overflowing physical energy.

Some children need a well-defined physical space — space they can retreat to when things aren't going well or a safe spot for being alone or calming down. Some children benefit from a shortened daily schedule or time spent in another classroom in which the peer or adult dynamics are different. The possibilities are numerous when we are truly responsive to individual needs and strengths. I find that even I must go back to my circle of support — the friends, family members, and colleagues who listen to me when I need to be heard. Sometimes they offer advice and suggestions or brainstorm possibilities; at other times they simply show empathy when I need their support.

# Barbara's mentor reflects . . .

Respect, trust, communication, conflict resolution, and responsibility are core components of positive guidance. Learning to understand children's behavior and become flexible enough to respond in a variety of positive ways is an ongoing process in teaching. Most of us can think of some past interaction with a child that we'd do differently if we could.

Barbara's account shows the value in rethinking such interactions as a productive way of developing new skills in guiding young children. She reflects carefully on the many factors that impact children's social and emotional growth.

Studies have shown that children's skills of coping and resiliency are affected by their relationships both with family members and with others outside the family, such as teachers, caregivers, or other concerned adults. A child's opportunity to form a caring, consistent relationship with an adult is pivotal in determining the child's present and future well-being.

Children do not leave their life experiences at the classroom door when the day begins. Understanding that worried, upset, or stressed children need additional support in the classroom environment, Barbara takes this as one of her vital responsibilities as a teacher. Rather than assume that children should be ready for her environment, she makes persistent efforts to create environments suitable for each child's unique needs; in other words, she works to make the environment ready for children.

Barbara's recollections remind us that understanding the reasons for children's actions needs to be at the core of our response to their behavior. When children have experienced trauma, their behavior is often drastically affected. As Barbara describes, we seek to learn more about a child to help him cope with the new environment and develop new strengths and skills.

Learning about children and reflecting on one's own practice can be difficult and sometimes painful. Teachers invest much of themselves in the classroom. Barbara expresses her conviction that every teacher needs to develop supports. She gains emotional support that guides and acknowledges her efforts in teaching. A circle of support enables her to further her understanding of children's behavior and enhance her role in providing positive guidance.

**T**hink about someone in your life who influenced your approach to guidance of young children or your feelings about guidance. Review what this person said or did that influenced you. In what ways are you similar to this person? In what ways do you think you are different?

**R**elate one of your own guidance success stories. Make a list of what you learned from this experience and ways to apply this knowledge to your current classroom. For one month write down each day one positive guidance technique you used in the classroom and deposit it in a large envelope. At the end of the month, share the techniques with a colleague and ask for feedback.

**C**reate your own slogan for children in the classroom or a bumper sticker that reflects your philosophy. Think about how you foster this idea in your classroom. Are any of your practices at odds with this slogan?

## Resources for further exploration of this topic

### Books and periodicals

Easton, M. 1997. Positive discipline: Fostering the self-esteem of young children. *Young Children* 52 (6): 43–46.

Gartrell, D. 1997. Beyond discipline to guidance. *Young Children* 52 (6): 34–42.

Honig, A.S. 1992. *Prosocial development in children: Caring, helping, and cooperating.* New York: Garland.

Marion, M. 1998. *Guidance of young children.* Columbus, OH: Charles Merrill.

Slaby, R.G., W.C. Roedell, D. Arezzo, & K. Hendrix. 1995. *Early violence prevention: Tools for teachers of young children.* Washington, DC: NAEYC.

Stone, J.G. 1978. *A guide to discipline.* Rev. ed. Washington, DC: NAEYC.

### Videotapes

*How to set limits.* 1991. Produced by Carolyn Webster-Stratton. 30 min. Seattle, WA: Parents and Children Series (1411 8th Ave. West, Seattle 98119; 202-285-7565).

*Painting a positive picture: Proactive behavior management.* 1994. Indiana Steps Ahead series. 28 min. Washington, DC: NAEYC.

South Carolina Educational Television. 1988. *Discipline: Appropriate guidance of young children.* 28 min. Washington, DC: NAEYC.

### Websites

Ask NOAH About: Mental Health—http://www.noah.cuny.edu/illness/mentalhealth/mental.html

The Council for Exceptional Children—http://www.cec.sped.org

The Educational Resources Information Center—http://ww.aspensys.com/eric/

Help Children Work with Feelings—http://www.aha4kids.com/index.html

National Association for the Education of Young Children—http://www.naeyc.org

National Child Care Information Center—http://nccic.org

National Parent Information Network—http://www.npin.org

### Community contacts

Consult your local mental health agency, state university extension program, or child abuse prevention organizations for information and workshops.

# Individualizing 3

*Susan Pieples and Mary Lowe*
*with Jan Jewett as mentor*

**W**e all benefit from being known as individuals, with unique strengths, limitations, and needs. It is tempting in our demanding lives as teachers to establish a routine or structure and then expect all children to adhere to it. Once we do so, however, we bump into issues of individuality and inclusion—what happens when some children are unable to keep up or function within the structure we have set. Because children are very different in what they are able to do, we must individualize the supports we give so as to help all children function well in the group and develop to their full potential.

Learning when and how to individualize requires experience and reflection. With each new group of children, we need time to get to know each child. We also need to know ourselves as individuals, including our own values, attitudes, and dispositions. These qualities help form the basis of our teaching decisions: how to act, what priorities to set, and what goals to pursue. Often these elements are a subconscious part of the foundation each person has laid in her own development. To make known clearly the deeply held values and dispositions that guide our teaching behaviors, we need self-exploration and reflection.

Another issue teachers face when individualizing is the issue of equity. With limited time, energy, attention, and resources, each teacher knows that he must make constant decisions about how to be fair to all the individuals in his group. Teachers must balance the many needs and concerns that come to them and also take precautions not to overtax their own inner resources. Our struggle to accomplish this task in an equitable way touches core values and beliefs about what *is* fair and just.

Individualizing requires knowledge, skills, and self-awareness. Reflecting on individual children and how they interact with our own individuality sustains our ability to provide this crucial quality in our work as teachers.

**Susan Pieples** says that she chose this topic because "one role of the Montessori teacher is to constantly reevaluate the process, and I saw this as the opportunity to do that—to look at what I was doing in the classroom and why." Susan describes the Montessori method as "so individual—creating curriculum for each and every child." Reflecting gave her the chance, she says, "to stop and focus on what I was doing with several of the individuals in my class." **Mary Lowe** chose to write about individualizing, she said, "because of the struggles I was having in trying to meet the needs of the diverse group I had. I wanted to reflect on what I was doing and learn from what worked and what didn't."

—Jan Jewett

Susan Pieples

I am more and more aware of how *individual* children can be. This awareness is especially poignant to me this school year as I stretch to include in our classroom two children with out-of-the-ordinary learning needs. Five-year-old Charles has Down syndrome. His younger brother Phil, who is 3½, started our program with very little language and frequent temper tantrums. In addition to these two children, my assistant and I teach 18 others whose ages range from 2½ to 6.

Having always wanted to teach, I found the Montessori philosophy so compelling and natural that I knew this was my course. For me, the Montessori approach means allowing the child to be self-driven, to unfold according to her own unique desires and needs. As the teacher, my role is to guide children, to observe and record, and to prepare the environment. Sometimes I need to invite or spark a child's engagement with a certain activity. And sometimes it is necessary to be firm with the child who is not yet showing self-control in a given situation.

This year when I learned we had the opportunity to take Charles into our class, I was very excited. I believed he could gain a lot from interacting with and observing the other children. I was also convinced that the other children would benefit from having him in the classroom. I did some reading over the summer to learn how other Montessori programs had responded to children with special needs. The best results appeared to be gained in classes like ours, where most of the children were developing typically and only a few had special needs. Although I was enthusiastic, I did have some concerns about Phil and Charles. For instance, I wondered whether the brothers would be too attached to one another to become well integrated into the group.

As a Montessori teacher, one of my primary functions is to observe the nature of each child's learning interests and to prepare the environment with materials and activities that stimulate and encourage that child to challenge himself in a natural progression of self-acquired knowledge and skills. In the Montessori curriculum the activities designed for children are termed *jobs*. Many activities, such as sorting and building activities, are familiar in various early childhood

**Susan Pieples** has been a Montessori teacher for the past six years in Carmel, Indiana.

programs, while others are unique to Montessori. From the jobs available on shelves, children choose the materials they wish to use and then engage in activity that Montessori describes as *work*. Jobs promote self-discipline and demonstrate respect for children's abilities.

My challenge this year was to provide materials that were meaningful to Charles, Phil, and each of the children in the classroom. But in a classroom that emphasizes individual self-discipline, I was deeply concerned about the presence of children who have not been able to regulate themselves. Does setting a different standard send a conflicting message to the children who do use self-control? Is a double standard necessary? What are the other options? My experience up to this point did not give me clear answers to these questions. And although my advance thinking about individualizing had focused on Phil and Charles, I found they were not the only children who caused me to examine my beliefs and practices about individualizing.

## Learning from the exceptions

In January I finished a week of parent conferences that by and large went well. Most parents were not surprised by what I had to say about their child's performance in the classroom. However, there was one exception —Justin's conference.

Four-year-old Justin had been in my classroom last year too. A highly energetic and very happy child, he was very fond of socializing, which is typical of a 4-year-old in our environment. But Justin seemed determined to avoid work. When invited to join an activity, he declined to come; when told to come, he refused and went in the opposite direction. In working with another child, he tried hard to distract the friend from the task at hand. Often he preferred make-believe play. He would head the other way when he saw me coming.

I did not discuss this behavior with the parents until conference time in January. Partly, I told myself, this was because I wanted to see if the worrisome behaviors persisted. However, I also was struggling in my own mind about my expectations for Justin — could I always distinguish between productive activity and nonproductive activity? And what should I do about it?

Justin's parents were very upset that they had not heard these things from me sooner. They were even more disturbed that I did not have a plan of action to keep him from avoiding his work on tasks. I felt I had failed because I allowed Justin to follow his own course of action rather than working to guide him in a new direction. It was very difficult for me for a few days. I worried that the parents would withdraw Justin from our school, and I felt responsible. As I thought about Justin and what *he* wanted, several thoughts came to mind. He appeared to want vividly imaginative play. He sought lots of interaction with one or two close friends. And he wanted to avoid failure.

I decided to try some ways to make learning less risky and more appealing for Justin and observe closely how he reacted. One day I invited Justin to get involved in lantern making and reluctantly he came. After I had demonstrated the method, I invited him to be the first person to make the lantern, but he refused. I encouraged Justin to make one to take home to show his mom and dad, but he was not interested. I suggested that he come back later and show lantern making to one of his friends. After about 30 minutes, another child came to me wanting a demonstration. I used this opportunity to approach Justin. I told him that his friend wanted to see the lantern

job, and we would both appreciate it if he could show her how to do it. Justin came without reluctance, but once he began he seemed hesitant. Although he was doing fine, he seemed very worried about his performance. I continued to look for ways to support Justin's engagement in activities and his sticking with them. I made an effort to get Justin to work on at least one Montessori task or lesson each day and to use the materials immediately following the lesson whenever possible. I tried to avoid the "you are here to work" speech. Instead, I mixed direct efforts to involve Justin with encouragement and support. I wrote a letter to his parents every week for a month to let them know how he was progressing.

In the following month, Justin and I worked together to use a variety of materials and to master several tasks. These included counting, literacy, and fine-motor activities. I also observed how his day played out when he was left to his own devices. I found that he worked closely with a friend, got involved in fantasy activity around the jobs, and used open-ended materials. During this time, he demonstrated an eagerness to progress to new challenges. His overall attitude seemed much more positive, and he showed less reluctance to take on new jobs. At the same time he expressed to his mother, "Mom, I just don't like jobs."

Then Justin hit a period in which he showed much better impulse control. He chose jobs of his own accord, and his concentration on tasks was longer and more focused. The usual play and pretend games with the other children into which he had previously put so much energy declined. But I resolved to spend the week watching Justin and trying to determine through observation what he was interested in during his spontaneous play. I have been getting interested in the functions it could have for his learning and development and eager to see how other teachers use play in their classrooms.

## With inclusion, new challenges

In the beginning, having Charles and Phil in our classroom was a real challenge. For the first two weeks, I was afraid I had made a terrible mistake in attempting to create an inclusive classroom. Having very little language, 3-year-old Phil screamed when he wanted something, and anything new seemed to terrify him.

When he screamed, I could see in his face great frustration at not being able to communicate his needs. To reduce the screaming, my assistant and I worked to give him words to use. I could see relief in his face, his eyes searching mine for understanding. Everything I did with and for Phil was intuitive. No diagnosis had been made; no one

I saw that what works for Michael
or Tom does not work for Phil.
Phil responds to a firm
"No!"

knew exactly what was wrong; and I
had no real training in special education.

As weeks went by, Phil gradually acquired
a few key phrases that enabled him to find security
in the classroom. "Want to come?" he would say when he
wanted to join us. He did not seem to understand pronouns and
repeated what was said to him (echolalia): "Don't touch!" "Wash
hands!" "Hi, Phil!" "Use the potty!" "Wait, Phil!" "No hands!" Yet the
more phrases he acquired, the less screaming he used. By the end of
six weeks, he rarely screamed.

Coming happily into the classroom, Phil went about his routine,
which varied little from day to day. He really concentrated on the jobs
he chose and seemed to be learning joyously from them. Displaying
an excellent memory, he learned the names of the geometrical solids
by listening as my assistant taught them to other children. And in only
two lessons, Phil learned the first six sounds of the Montessori alpha-
bet sandpaper letters, which are cut from sandpaper and glued on
wood blocks over which children move their fingers while practicing
the letter sound out loud. He now knows the words to every song
we've ever sung in class. Being introduced to a new job or having his
routine changed is still difficult for Phil, but we are feeling our way
and finding creative ways of helping him handle change.

## Individualizing by attending to needs

There is a lot to learn about individual differences, but I believe
there's also a lot to be said for trusting our common sense. We can
begin with thinking about what each child needs and how to provide
it each day. We must not be too afraid of making a mistake. If I mis-
judge what Phil needs but keep trying, eventually I will find what
works. If I don't try because of my fear, then neither of us grows.

Phil needs more direct discipline than we usually use in the Montessori environment. At first it was hard for me to justify my treating
him differently. But I saw that what works for Michael or Tom does
not work for Phil. Phil responds to a firm "No!" When I am less firm
and clear, he fails to respond. Without that firmness Phil gets out of
control, and soon the whole classroom is unrestrained. The other
children seem to understand that Phil needs different treatment. I was
surprised to learn that the other children accept both Phil and his
brother Charles for who they are. The children are eager to help,
perhaps too much so sometimes, but by and large they treat the boys
as equals and work hard to enable them to succeed. Although the
children recognize that Phil and Charles have different abilities than

they themselves have, these differences don't separate them. The children include the boys in all that we do and accept the necessary adjustments in our routine to accommodate their needs.

Of course some social problems occur. Phil seems to have only a limited sense of the other children as distinct from one another. He can identify one girl who mothered him early on. He knows his brother and will hug and then wrestle with Charles. He relates to both teachers, although he responds better to my assistant, who has worked more with him. He seems to look past the other children and tries to hit them if they get in his way. He tries to take their work and does not respect personal space as other children his age do. Between the moment someone says something to Phil and the moment he grasps it, there is typically a long delay. This creates difficulty in his interacting with the other children since they usually don't give him enough time to process what they say. I've noticed a kind of mockery or repetition of Phil's and Charles's language patterns by the older children. Phil began to use the expression "Go away," and now I realize that it came from the other children telling him to do so. One of my concerns is how we can work as a group to find new words or actions for dealing with behavior when others disturb our work.

## Inclusion and individualizing

I believe the inclusion of Justin, Phil, and Charles has been a good learning experience for everyone. I think our lessons are just beginning, for we can learn as much from our questions as from a textbook.

I have just begun to work with the children on recognizing our differences. We sat together at circle time one day, and I posed some questions: How are we different from each other? How am I different from you? Then I explained to the children that one way in which I am different from them is that I am a mom and none of them is. Gradually they came up with differences in gender, hair color, eyes, skin color, language, and so on. We now have the basis for a discussion about the differences in how we learn and how Phil and Charles are learning from their peers in this environment.

Should children know that they have a responsibility for what their peers learn from them? We use this kind of language in talking with children about not using "bad" words or "bad" behavior, so perhaps we can take this further and talk about the good things that we learn from each other.

Charles has made some notable gains recently in the acquisition of phonics and in small-motor skills. He is showing interest in doing a greater range of tasks as well as looking at books or watching the other children. For example, he has chosen sewing, cutting with

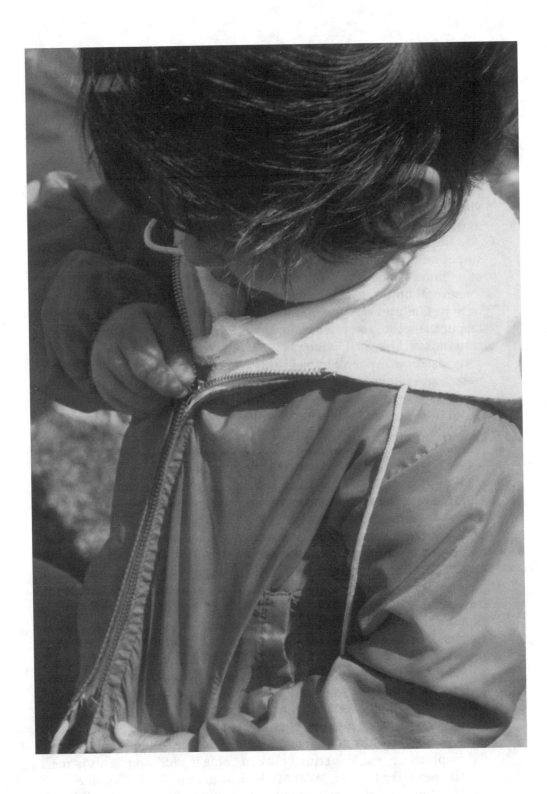

scissors, baby washing, and a job using a bulb syringe. I need to take time with him when he is working on scissors skills and sewing, but he is benefiting from this practice of skills.

## Strategies for individualizing

Sometimes I realize I can plan and plan and still have to wait for the right moment for certain learning to take place. For weeks I tried to interest Phil in counting. I knew he could count to 20 by rote, but I was unsure if he understood number. Every attempt to entice him into a counting job was met with screams or "Go away!"

One day Phil was exploring a new shelf and found a basket of stones and two pitchers that we sometimes use in introducing the idea of addition. He was very attracted to the stones and remained attentive for several minutes just feeling the smooth, blue glass stones. I quietly went to him and showed him how to count the stones one at a time as he put them into the pitcher. At first we did this without taking the materials off the shelf, which is not what we usually do in a Montessori classroom. When Phil was fully captivated, I carefully moved the basket and pitchers to a nearby table. He followed and sat right down.

Phil's movements were not as careful as mine; he would pick up a fistful of stones and still count them as one, so I would take stones from his fistful until he had only one. We repeated this activity over and over, counting as we went.

Phil developed one activity that became special for him. On the shelf in the language area was a basket of individual photos of the children that the school photographer had given us. We were using it to say the names of the children and talk about the beginning sounds of each person's name. Phil discovered this basket and became totally enthralled. Every day when he came in, he would take the basket and search through it until he found his picture and his brother's. I observed this process for several days and decided to try extending the activity. Phil found his brother's photo and said to me, "This is Charles." Then he found his own picture, and he said, "This is Phil." He has consistently referred to himself in the third person and doesn't seem to understand how to use *me* or *I*. I spent the next 15 minutes telling him, "This is me." I engaged the other children in finding their own pictures and each saying, "This is me." I used every opportunity Phil gave me to repeat these words. At first he looked at me and seemed confused. But I knew that he does imitate what he hears, and I thought that perhaps I could teach him to use *me*. After 15 minutes he did begin to use *me*, wavering between "This is Phil" and "This is me."

The next day he said, "Want to look at pictures?" He took the basket again, and this time he spoke right away, "This is me." Phil got lots of positive feedback from me, and I enlisted the help of the other children. Later Phil went over to the mirror in the classroom, and I stood behind him and said, "This is me." He continued to work on the photos and the phrase for four days. He doesn't fully grasp the way the pronoun works yet, but this experience was a step forward.

With Phil I often have to wait until he is willing to connect with me. When the time is right, I must be ready to pick up on the opportunity to interact. This effort has been a challenge, but it is rewarding when I see that he makes progress. Thinking back on the first two weeks of school when Phil had no words and spent much of the time mindlessly screaming and running from one place to another, I am astounded that he functions today with so many understandable phrases and an impressive attention span. His memory capability is striking. And his joy makes me want to continue trying harder to reach him.

When I talked with Phil's speech teacher last week, she expressed encouragement and complimented the work we have been doing with Phil at our school. She suggested that I continue the work with the photographs and use the mirror in having Phil point to himself when saying, "This is me." We also talked about engaging all of the children in playing the Good Afternoon game. In this whole-group activity, children take turns saying, "Good afternoon," calling each other by name so that Phil can learn that each child has a different name and how to use those names appropriately. Phil enjoyed the game, and every day when we would start, he would get a big grin on his face and have a hard time waiting for his turn to come around the circle. Sometimes our progress seems slow, but Phil has made great strides since school began.

## Play and individuality

During this time of adjustment, I joined another class in the Best Practices project, which focused on the theme of play. Play has been a big issue for me, especially because of recent events with Justin. I feel a need to reevaluate the role of play in my classroom. I have ordered two books on the subject in which I plan to immerse myself. I have listened closely when the leader of this class talks about her own experiences with children's play in the classroom and how much children benefit from their play, especially emotionally.

From yesterday's seminar, I came away with an important new thought for me — in evaluating children and their progress it would be more fair and productive to look at what they can do and how they do it than to focus on what they cannot do. We read the story "Animal School," in which all kinds of different animals are subjected to the same curriculum and expected to do everything the same way. Of course, each one fails. By looking at every child and his or her characteristics as a complete package, I can better individualize my instruction. Indeed, we are all individuals with unique ways of seeing, hearing, expressing — learning.

If it is important to understand Phil's current language limitations, it is no less important to understand Justin's attraction to play activities outside the usual Montessori jobs that I may have in mind. How limiting for us both if I ignore what he is doing or try to override or ignore his own initiatives and self-development to adhere to my own advance judgment of what he needs! After all, Maria Montessori argued that children have a strong sense of what they need and are ready to learn. It is often adults who get in the way.

The combination of these ideas — first, seeing differences among children as a fact of life and, second, recognizing the child's capabilities and supporting these rather than comparing them — has begun to have a dramatic impact on my thinking. I still have work to do in examining and changing my old biases about play. When I next do conferences with parents, I know I will give them feedback differently. I will be focusing every day on my observation of the children from a new perspective, and I believe that they will be the better for it. The animal story reminds us that we cannot mass produce one education formula well suited to all.

## Reflections on individual progress

Near the end of December, Justin brought to school a set of cards with three- and four-letter words written on them, all using the *a* sound. He was very eager to read them to me, and his mother delightedly told me he had read them in the car all the way to school. He did a wonderful job of reading about 20 cards before he tired. Several other children gathered around, and some of the older ones were eager to help Justin when he came to a letter he did not recognize. Since he hadn't been spending much time on reading-related activities here in class, I was surprised at what he could do. I let him know we had similar jobs here at school if he wanted to continue his work with letters and sounds.

So, Justin has begun to read. His apprehension about jobs has faded. Emotionally he seems to have grown about a year's worth in three months. Often the changes in children seem so dramatic from January to May. A major concern one week completely vanishes the following week. To an amazing degree, children seek what they need and are ready for. One of the most important things we can do is watch, listen to, and follow the child.

Both Charles and Phil have come a long way in their use of language. Phil's ability to use pronouns, for example, continues to improve. Today he asked me, "Will you tie my pants?" "Will you push me?" And recently he said, "I came in this door!"

Seeing the rapid gains these three children have made in language and reading skills has been remarkable. Two years ago I don't think I could have dealt with this challenge. I was too keen on giving lessons, ensuring that children followed certain tracks, and keeping them constantly busy. As I have matured and developed confidence in my teaching, I also have gained respect for children's natural inclinations. And I often find that the ones who seem the least busy are the most involved in learning, because their learning is through observation. I have learned to respect what children are choosing to do, especially their play.

I'll close with my belief that even experienced teachers still need to use trial and error. At times what we try works and at other times it does not. What didn't work yesterday works today. The success I have had has depended largely on my intuition and willingness to take risks. Children continually challenge us and our beliefs. From facing these challenges, reflecting on my practices, and interacting with other teachers who share their reflections, I continue to learn.

# Susan's mentor reflects . . .

The Montessori approach has a strong emphasis on individualizing. Teachers use their understandings about individual children's growth patterns, learning characteristics, interests, and experiences to help each child grow and develop to his or her full potential.

Susan prepared in several ways to work with children like Charles and Phil, whose abilities and behaviors differed from those of children she was used to. One way she did this was to acquaint herself with the knowledge base about what works for children with particular disabilities. She also talked with other adults who work with these children. Susan asked herself some core questions that all educators address in individualizing teaching: How do we treat children fairly if we can't treat them all the same way? If we set more modest expectations for certain children, are we shortchanging them or the rest of the children?

Susan's work with Justin taught her a lot about individualizing. Her efforts to understand his style of learning led to her learning more about play. Traditional Montessori programs do not emphasize play in the same way that many early childhood programs do. Susan also had to examine her own beliefs and values about learning. At first she defined *work* as those activities she wanted to encourage and *play* as any distraction from that. Later she reassessed her assumptions about what constitutes productive activity for a child.

For all teachers questions arise about productive activity and how to set individually appropriate expectations. Goals and expectations for progress or productive activity come from several sources: knowledge of child development, adults' values and beliefs about what is important and appropriate for children to learn and develop, and knowledge of each child's unique strengths and characteristics. Grappling with her questions, Susan drew from each of these sources.

Observation is essential to individualizing. Susan observed children's behavior and reflected on her interactions with the children. She used record keeping to help her understand children as individuals, keep track of their progress, and give her a sound basis for communicating with their families. Being clear about children's achievements is key, assisting us in knowing when and how to encourage or challenge individual children and in informing their families and other professionals of the child's progress and the areas where further work is needed.

Susan's writing conveys another key concept in supporting all children: incremental progress. Phil's progress occurs at a slower pace and in a different pattern than Susan was used to. Teacher, child, and parents benefit when the teacher identifies the small but critical steps the child is making in his development and when she continues to encourage him by setting and supporting appropriate expectations.

At times, each of us confronts situations in our work for which we feel unprepared. Gaining additional knowledge and training helps us develop new skills and handle the stress of unfamiliar challenges. Making a point of paying attention to individual children and working to communicate with them are essential. Susan helped Phil by providing a safe, supportive structure with consistent expectations and routines. These supports provided the security Phil needed to show his strengths and capabilities and express himself more positively. Susan's efforts to meet Phil's individual needs resulted in a satisfying, productive teacher-child relationship.

Ask yourself this question: Does treating all children fairly mean treating them the same? Think about your own experiences. Ask other colleagues this question. How do they deal with this issue?

List or otherwise represent your strengths. Think about the ways in which you do or do not exercise these strengths. How can you build on your strengths? In a group, list your collective strengths. Consider how being in a group enhances and challenges you.

On a sheet of paper folded in half, write on one half your needs as a teacher. On the other half write the needs of a child in your classroom whose situation challenges you. With others in a small group, brainstorm ways to balance these needs.

# Mary Lowe

Mary Lowe

My afternoon developmental preschool class could have come right out of one of those made-for-TV movies starring a Sally Field type as the virtuous special education teacher who, with her gentle and caring ways, works miracles with the out-of-control children. This class made me feel it could chew me up and spit me out in 10 seconds; it exposed every chink in my armor. Nightly the class sent me home dejected, exhausted, in tears, and with fresh battle scars. This class made me wonder, after 15 years of teaching, if I had the tenacity to continue teaching.

I teach what is termed *developmental preschool* in a large urban public school system. My class serves only children with special needs and is a self-contained, multicategorical classroom within a Montessori public school. Because of funding cuts some years ago, there are no opportunities for inclusion with typically developing peers. Therein lies a philosophical and ethical struggle I deal with daily. What is best for these children? Will they learn more in our isolated classroom or would they benefit from being with their peers in an inclusive setting? On most days I will argue that these children need the language and socialization models provided by their typically developing peers. On other days, I feel that as a special educator, I can provide the best education for the small group of children in this self-contained classroom, where I can create a safe, nurturing environment.

I have always been a special education teacher with my own special classroom. If my children are included in a regular classroom, I wonder, what becomes of me? Yet I truly believe that children learn best from their peers in an inclusive setting. If children with special needs have only each other as models, we set them up for failure. What often results is an out-of-control classroom with very little learning going on. Teaching becomes a daily battle of damage control just to keep everyone safe and able to go home in one piece. This picture sets the background for the scenario of my afternoon class this September.

*Mary Lowe, M.S., was a preschool and elementary school teacher for many years. Currently she is a member of the early childhood evaluation team and a resource teacher in community-based preschool programs in Indianapolis.*

## Seven children

If children with special needs have only each other as models, we set them up for failure.

Everyone in school referred to this class as The Wild Ones. The group consisted of seven 3- to 6-year-old boys. Each child had his own needs and demands, which often exceeded what I felt that my classroom assistant and I could handle. Roberto had a hearing impairment, wore bilateral hearing aids, and had been shifted from the care of one family member to another in his few short years. Prone to daily temper tantrums, complete with self-induced vomiting when he felt a loss of control, Roberto demonstrated very low self-esteem. Chris had craniostenosis, a malformation of the skull, and had severe mental disabilities. He tended to scream, grind his teeth, and cling to the adults in the classroom.

Daniel had Fragile X syndrome and exhibited many autistic characteristics as well as hyperactivity. Six-year-old Neal, diagnosed with severe autism, was in school for the first time. He spent his time juggling various items and climbing on furniture. Marco was severely mentally disabled and had several difficult behaviors, including throwing toys on the floor and spitting on the adults. Though I hated to admit it, I was having trouble liking him. Matthew had mild mental disabilities and preferred to spend most of his day at the computer. Then there was Ronnie. With severe autism, Ronnie had a very difficult time adjusting to the environment of our classroom. Physically large for a 3-year-old and prone to physical aggression — kicking, hitting, biting, and pinching — Ronnie was by far the most challenging child in the class. He was the one who seemed to take much of my time away from the other boys, time they all desperately needed.

## Allocating time and affection

Spending so much time with one child while the rest of my class was left to my assistant troubled me. The other boys often were left to entertain themselves as we continually put out fires. Just trying to keep everyone safe seemed to be the main goal of each day. It became frustrating and demoralizing for both of us.

A typical day in the classroom was like a surreal journey into the Twilight Zone. The boys would come to school full of energy. We could tell how active the day would be as soon as the boys got off the bus. If Roberto had a glare on his face, a temper tantrum was on the way. When we saw Daniel come literally bouncing off the bus like Tigger in *Winnie the Pooh*, we knew we would spend the day following him around as he grabbed one activity after another. Chris would slowly make his way down the aisle of the bus wanting to be held; Marco would run off the bus, laughing and seeking attention, while

Neal screamed and jumped up and down. Waking Matthew from his nap on the bus, we knew he would play alone all day, withdrawing from the other children. Ronnie would begin crying as soon as he set eyes on us. It took all of our energy and will to take those children off the bus each day. I think we both said silent prayers as we went out to greet the children each day, and when one boy was absent, we gave a sigh of relief for this small reprieve.

As soon as coats were hung up, it was time for lunch — a phenomenon in itself. We ate during the same lunch period as the fourth and fifth graders, who rolled their eyes as the "babies" came into the cafeteria. Roberto often cried and sometimes even threw up if we couldn't help him right away to open his milk or cold drink. Marco climbed under the table looking for scraps of food. Neal stood on the bench juggling straws and screaming. Daniel might stuff a whole sandwich into his mouth and then try to run out into the hall, while Chris screamed at the top of his lungs. And Ronnie might cry, hit, bite, or scream and run around the cafeteria — an environment not conducive to enjoying lunch.

After lunch we returned to the classroom for circle time and daily activities. Circle time consisted of five minutes of greetings, a look at the day's schedule, counting, and a song. But Roberto, Matthew, and

Daniel were the only ones who seemed able to sit and pay attention. Marco, Neal, Ronnie, and Chris usually were off doing their own thing.

## Struggling alone

Next it was time for one-on-one instruction, individualized learning plans, and choice time. Most things fell apart at this point in the day. How, I wonder, does one individualize and provide quality instruction in the midst of pandemonium?

I feared that my afternoons might be this way for the rest of the year. I needed help desperately. At first I was too proud to seek it. I have a reputation for being a good teacher who enjoys working with children who exhibit challenging behaviors. It's very hard to live up to such high expectations. How could I admit to people I know and respect that I couldn't handle this? I worried about saying, "I don't know what to do."

Not surprisingly, the class was taking a toll on my personal life. I was short tempered with my family. I slept poorly at night, tossing and turning, worrying about what I could do to meet the needs of each of these very complex young boys. I dreaded going to work each day, and I had never felt that way before. I considered changing to a different area of special education or even leaving teaching altogether.

I continued to try to adapt the schedule, try new strategies, adapt some more, go with the flow, but nothing seemed to help. In fact, Ronnie was becoming more aggressive daily. Perhaps the changes I was making in the classroom set him off, or it may have been his reaction to all the chaos. One afternoon, he went so out of control that my principal heard the noise and popped in. She attempted to calm Ronnie, but he tried to bite her. Things were going from bad to worse.

## Talking to the child's mother

Desperate and recognizing that the person who knew Ronnie best was his mother, I arranged for a home visit to brainstorm some ideas with her. Ronnie's mother told me that he exhibited similar behaviors at home. She was firm with Ronnie and put him in time-out, where he was comforted by a bottle — probably not a good option for school — but this worked very well for her. I could see that Ronnie was different at home. Fairly calm throughout my visit, he seemed intrigued to see me at his house. Over the next six weeks, I made two more home visits to explore more strategies for helping Ronnie adjust to life at school. Meanwhile, the situation at school was getting worse instead of better. Ronnie spent most of the day crying, leading us to the door, and biting, hitting, and scratching. He also was beginning to lash out at the other boys in the classroom. He appeared to be communicating his wish: "Get me the heck out of here!"

Working with children with autism is usually satisfying for me. I love finding the keys that enable me to communicate more effectively with them. With Ronnie, however, even my best skills were not cracking these locks. I felt frustrated; I know Ronnie was even more so.

## Getting help

Shortly before the school break in December, Ronnie's behavior reached the max. He was fully out of control — crying, hitting, and biting. Being unable to communicate to us what he wanted had to be very scary and frustrating for him. The physical therapist came to the classroom in an attempt to help calm Ronnie. We thought swaddling him in a blanket would be comforting, but he kicked and thrashed so much that we were unable to wrap him up. The school counselor heard the commotion as he walked by and came in to offer some assistance. Ronnie shoved him into a bookshelf, upsetting all the toys. The speech therapist, who had come for her weekly visit, also attempted to calm Ronnie. When he tried to bite her, she shifted to the other boys to keep them busy. The consulting teacher too came in to offer help.

By this time the classroom had adult overload, and Ronnie's distress was rising. Finally he stopped crying, out of sheer exhaustion more than anything else, but not before the principal arrived. I knew she was upset. She is supportive of everything I do in my classroom and often offers an extra hand when needed, even changing diapers in a pinch. On this day she took one look and said, "This is it, Mary, no more! I cannot jeopardize your safety or that of these children any more. Ronnie has to go!" I felt my control go and started sobbing uncontrollably. She wrapped her arms about me and said, "It's not you, Mary. We just need to try something else with Ronnie for a while."

But I wasn't hearing what she was saying. In my mind I heard, "You are a failure. You should have been able to figure out some way to calm Ronnie down and control your classroom." I couldn't stop crying. Part of my reaction was a response to the stress of the last few months. Our consulting teacher, a personal friend, tried to reassure me, but I still felt that I could have done something to make a difference for Ronnie.

I was concerned too about how Ronnie's parents would feel. I know that besides our educational role, we teachers provide respite to parents of children whose care is very demanding. How could we deny these parents that support? The principal telephoned Ronnie's mother to say that we needed to hold a multidiciplinary team meeting

Besides our educational role, we teachers provide respite to parents of
children whose care is
very demanding.

to determine the best help for Ronnie.
His mother was very open to the suggestion. The team met at her home the next day.
As a team we decided that homebound instruction
was the best thing for the time being.

I felt strongly that I should be the teacher who provided Ronnie's
homebound instruction, but others questioned whether, emotionally,
this was appropriate. My peers believed that I needed a break from
Ronnie. I was convinced, however, that if Ronnie were to come back
into our classroom this year, he needed to trust and feel comfortable
with someone who linked him to that environment. I needed to be that
person to provide continuity for Ronnie. I also needed to prove to
myself that I could make a difference for him and was a good teacher.
I offered to use my lunch hour each day to teach Ronnie on his home
turf. The next month was a turning point for both Ronnie and me.

## Trying a new approach

On my first visit Ronnie was little interested in what I had brought
him to do. He spent half the time running to hide in his parents'
bedroom or being comforted by his bottle. He sat on his mother's lap
about five minutes while she helped him, hand over hand, to manipulate the materials. When my time was up he ran into the hallway but
popped his head around the corner as I went out the door. The next
day was the same, except that he stayed in the living room when I left.
On the third day Ronnie took my hand when I started to leave. I was
on cloud nine.

Over the next few weeks in January and February, Ronnie became
much more attentive to the materials I brought and began to work
with some of them without the hand-over-hand instruction required in
the beginning. He also was becoming comfortable with me. A major
breakthrough occurred the day that he greeted me with a hug and a
kiss on my cheek. Excited that we might be beginning to unlock
Ronnie's world, I told everyone at school and even called the consultant to tell her that we were over the hump in reaching Ronnie.

## Other individuals emerge

Meanwhile, with Ronnie's absence, the atmosphere in the classroom was somewhat calmer. I hadn't realized the impact of his behavior on the whole classroom, including the behaviors of the other boys.
Everyone had felt the stress. Although the setting still seemed fairly

chaotic, we were able to give more time and energy to the other boys. I hadn't been aware of just how much time and attention Ronnie took. I regretted not having provided the best for the other children in the classroom. A little more time from a less-stressed teacher proved to be the best medicine for us all.

Roberto had fewer temper tantrums and began playing more with Matthew. His self-confidence was building as he became adept at the computer and a whiz at playing Memory. I played with him each day, and he delighted in beating me every time (and I really tried to remember where those pairs were!). He no longer fussed about wearing his hearing aids and took pride in his new job of getting the auditory trainer set up. He still had trying moments, but by and large he was a delight in the classroom.

Matthew started to come out of his shell and began talking more to all of us. He was proud that he could read everyone's name in the class and was the only one who could write his name. We sent home at least three paintings a day with MATTHEW emblazoned across the top. His smile could light a thousand candles.

Daniel remained very active, but we had more time for helping him stay focused on activities. He became curious about the computer and began requesting time to use it.

Marco was spending less time climbing, and he was getting engrossed in painting at the easel. Although he often inflexibly pursued one activity, such as painting everything in sight, he could be redirected to other tasks.

Although Neal still liked to juggle little bits of paper and straw, he was beginning to interact a bit. For instance, when he wanted to get my attention, he would come up behind and whack me on the back. He was starting to leave his self-absorbed world and become interested in the world of the classroom. He took delight in turning the lights on and off to remind us of time to clean up.

Daniel continued hanging onto the adults, but he began getting toys off the shelf and bringing them to us to help him play. He learned to manipulate a switch toy and took great delight in his newfound ability.

What were the keys to this turnaround? Was it that Ronnie was gone and our classroom was calmer? Had we reached that point in the year when progress is on the upswing? Was it that my assistant and I felt less stress? Was it that now we had more time to devote to the boys on an individual basis? I don't think there is one definitive answer.

### Feeling less alone

With the Autism Center at Indiana University we arranged a consultation about Ronnie in mid-January. I looked forward to some answers from the experts about the best way to help him. A center consultant visited Ronnie at home, which proved to be very helpful. After sufficient observation of Ronnie, we returned to school for the consultation, in which Ronnie's mother, the principal, and the consulting teacher participated. We discussed the ways autism affects Ronnie: his extreme reaction to change in routine, his limited awareness of others, his inability to communicate verbally, his fascination with waving and flipping objects such as straws and string, and his aggression toward others as means of communication.

Agreeing that it was important for Ronnie to get back into the routine of coming to school, we developed several strategies to help facilitate his reentry. Since the bus ride is a strong motivator for Ronnie, he would ride the bus to school. At first, he would stay for only 15 minutes each day and then be picked up by his mother or grandmother. I would develop a communication book for him to help him prepare for the routine he would follow. The process would take time and require consistency, but the eventual goal was having Ronnie attend the entire two-and-one-half-hour class session. Because the afternoon group was very demanding, we agreed that an extra assistant would be assigned to the classroom.

I left the consultation no longer feeling that I had let Ronnie down. I also felt that placing Ronnie on homebound instruction had been the best thing for him. He needed time to adjust to being away from his mother and time to establish a trusting relationship with me.

### Fostering reentry

On Monday I was full of anticipation and some trepidation. How would Ronnie respond? How would the other boys react to Ronnie being back? And how would we feel if he was unable to adjust? Getting off the bus with much energy, Ronnie acted as if he had never been away. I gave a sigh of relief. He entered the classroom, went straight to his favorite shelf, and got a piece of circular cardboard to flip. I helped him take off his coat and hang it on the hook.

The two classroom assistants took the other boys to the cafeteria to eat lunch. With our communication book, I showed Ronnie that it was time for us to work together. At the table, I had set out his favorite materials: a switch toy (an alligator that snaps its mouth open and closed), a jack-in-the-box, an activity box, and a spinning top. He eagerly sat on my lap and began to manipulate the switch on and off. He put his finger in the alligator's mouth and took my hand and tried to place it in the alligator's mouth. When the alligator bit my hand, I feigned injury with great animation. Ronnie leaned back and smiled while putting his cheek against mine. Tears began to well in my eyes. I couldn't believe what was happening. Ronnie was connecting with me and obviously feeling very comfortable in the classroom. What had made the difference? Why was he no longer so distressed? I think that my having come to Ronnie's own world to teach him had made me someone he could trust.

But it was good that we had decided to ease him back gradually. Five minutes before Ronnie's grandmother came to pick him up, he began to whimper. As soon as he saw her, he walked over to get his coat. Ronnie took my hand when he left and looked at me out of the corner of his eye, as if to tell me, "Hey, this isn't so bad after all!" or "You aren't so mean!" or simply "Thank you." After that successful first session, I knew Ronnie would be back with us full time before the school year was over. In the following weeks there were many signs of progress as well as some backslides. Usually he contentedly sat on my lap and worked with me, but some days he cried fretfully until a family member came to pick him up. His mom and grandma were convinced that on those days he was not feeling well. They knew Ronnie better than anyone else did, and I believed them. Indeed, they were proved right when he was admitted to the hospital with pneumonia.

I worried whether our class would experience a gigantic backslide on Ronnie's return to school, but my fears were disproved. His initial foray back into the classroom had been successful, and when Ronnie returned from his hospitalization ready to begin anew, it was as if he had never been away. He began to communicate more each day. One day he took my hand and led me to the water fountain. I immediately began to say, "Drink?" and "Ronnie wants drink?" Soon he began to lead each of us to the water fountain when he wanted a drink.

One day I showed Ronnie the picture of our work in his communication book and asked him to show me our work. He grabbed my hand and took me to the table where his work was. I was excited and gave him a big hug. He gave me a look like, "What's the big deal?"

As Ronnie opened up more each day, his interactions with his peers changed as well. He no longer acted aggressively toward the other boys. When he was upset, he separated himself from the rest of the children and came to one of the adults in the room.

As Ronnie was able to handle the routine, we began to increase his stay in the classroom by 15-minute increments. In two months

Ronnie was able to remain in class for an hour and a half. By the second week of April, Ronnie was coming to school the entire two and one-half hours.

### Reflecting on the process

What was the deciding factor that made possible the breakthrough with Ronnie? Although I'm not sure there is a definitive answer, it began with my approaching my teaching role differently. I had to stop trying to figure it all out myself. What helped us was listening to other people's ideas and looking at what really was best for Ronnie and the rest of the children.

This group of seven children taught me a lot about reflective thinking and learning to listen to the input of others. I began looking at how I had been structuring my classroom and wondering if what I was doing really was best for children.

It has always been hard for me to ask others for help. Even when I was in elementary school I didn't want to raise my hand for fear I would ask a stupid question or give a stupid answer. I guess it's been a matter of self-esteem: will others think less of me if I don't know the answers? But this challenging group of kids changed all of that for me. I realized that if I were to reach any of these children and make a difference, I needed to quit working in a vacuum and start listening to others. When the principal came into my classroom on that turning-point day when Ronnie was totally out of control, my whole being was called into question. To me it seemed that her decision to take him out of the class was a reflection on my teaching. But it was the best thing for Ronnie and for the rest us. The principal and the education consultant knew this, and I learned to see it was true. Sometimes we need others to show us the way.

It is so easy too to get into the groove of always doing things the same way. I had taught special education for 15 years, preschool for 4 years. It was time for me to take a fresh look at my teaching practices, not only for the children's sake, but for mine. Burnout and stagnation happen too easily in our profession. The very fact that I couldn't handle this group in my usual positive, calm way was a wake-up call that was overdue.

## Time for a change

How to change? The answer came to me in the middle of the night – sometimes my very best thinking time. Children often learn best from their peers, who model behaviors and actions. The boys in my class had only the adults and each other modeling. They needed typically developing peers to show them the way. Perhaps if these boys had had other children to observe, they could have seen that climbing on furniture and spitting on adults are not acceptable behaviors. They would see constructive, appropriate behaviors that they could adopt.

Next year we will open our classroom to typically developing peers from the neighborhood. We are looking forward to seeing how their presence affects the functioning of children with special needs and how they themselves respond. The trials and tribulations of this class of boys taught me an interesting lesson: teaching is an evolving process.

# Mary's mentor reflects . . .

Each of us encounters challenges in our work that can tax us to our limit. When Mary experienced such feelings, she had to examine her sense of self in relation to her very demanding work. The difficult dilemma she faced actually stimulated her reflection and growth. In the process, she developed an awareness of her beliefs and reactions to the circumstances in her classroom and to the way the school works as a whole, and she learned more about herself.

As she worked with Ronnie at home, Mary began to see that his early aggression and disruptive behavior were based in part on separation anxiety. Many children experience stress upon separation from their families, especially the first time. When children's perceptions and ways of communicating differ from those of typically developing children, their ways of showing separation stress are often harder for teachers to recognize and understand (Balaban 1986). Developing rapport with Ronnie and allowing him to become slowly acclimated to the school environment were important in responding to his separation anxiety and meeting his individual needs.

Mary's self-honesty and willingness to consider her own reactions to Ronnie opened the door for her to recognize his separation anxiety and difficulty dealing with change. Her reflection provided rich ground from which grew a much deeper understanding of Ronnie's needs and her own. We are only truly able to help children realize their full potential when we know and appreciate who they are as individuals. This understanding, in turn, grows out of trust and rapport. In going to his home and sticking by him, Mary gave Ronnie the security and acceptance he needed to build a relationship.

As Ronnie's anxiety lessened, his aggression decreased. Behaviors that challenge us often carry important messages, though these may be very difficult to understand and respond to. The support group around Ronnie responded to his needs through persistent and insightful efforts.

Though the stress in Mary's job was exceptionally high, all teachers struggle with job stress. Learning to manage stress and take care of their personal needs are essential for teachers. But learning to reflect on and reframe difficult situations are also crucial, enabling teachers to resolve or ease the problems that are causing the stress. Mary's writing illustrates the power of standing back and reframing a problem.

Meeting the child's individual needs requires more than the wisdom and skills of one individual. In working closely with Ronnie's family and consulting with other professionals, Mary learned more about his strengths and needs and benefited from their support and input.

Think about the educational philosophy of the school where you teach or observe. Are plans made in terms of individuals or simply for the group as a whole? Are children encouraged to work alone, in small groups, or in large groups? What does each of these modes contribute to children's development? What are the limitations of each?

Every week jot down on a note card one success of an individual child. Put each card into a large envelope. After several months review the notes and celebrate the successes.

Think about the support system you rely on when you are under a lot of job stress or in a quandary about a problem or decision in your work. Draw your support system, beginning with you in the middle, and then add a close circle of immediate support and other circles beyond. Are there gaps in your support system? If so, can you think of new ways to get support?

## References and resources for further exploration of this topic

### Books and articles

Balaban, N. 1985. *Starting school: From separation to independence.* New York: Teachers College Press.

Beardsley, L. 1990. *Good day/bad day: The child's experience of day care.* New York: Teachers College Press.

Johnson, L.J., M.J. LaMontagne, P.M. Elgas, & A.M. Bauer. 1998. *Early childhood education: Blending theory, blending practice.* Baltimore: Paul H. Brookes.

Paley, V.G. 1990. *The boy who thought he was a helicopter.* Cambridge, MA: Harvard University Press.

Read, K., P. Gardner, & B. Mahler. 1993. *Early childhood programs: A laboratory for human relations.* New York: Holt, Rinehart & Winston.

Tobin, L. 1991. *What do you do with a child like this? Inside the lives of troubled children.* Duluth, MN: Whole Person Associates.

### Videotapes

*I wish I were a princess.* Terry Strauss production. 17 min. San Francisco: Coleman Advocates for Children (415-641-4362).

*Love me and leave me: Attachment and independence.* Footsteps series. 28 min. College Park, MD: University of Maryland (Educational Technology Center, 0307 Benjamin Building, College Park, MD 20742). Shows how to make easier the separation between parent and child.

*No comparison: Individuality.* Footsteps series. 28 min. College Park, MD: University of Maryland (Educational Technology Center, 0307 Benjamin Building, College Park, MD 20742). Parents learn how to help children's growth and development.

### Websites

Children Now—http://www.childrennow.org
Classroom Connect—http://www.classroom.net/classroom
The Council for Exceptional Children—http://www.cec.sped.org
Help Children Work with Feelings—http://www.aha4kids.com/index.html
I Am Your Child—http://iamyourchild.org/

### Community contacts

Consult your college or university, local public and school libraries, and early childhood organizations for resources.

# Including Everyone 4

*Sherry Holliday and Diane Miller Parker*
*with Susan Klein as mentor*

**M**any of us grew up in a time when people whose appearance or behavior differed from the norm were avoided. As children we were taught to look the other way when we saw someone atypical and not to mention the differences we observed. Such individuals were kept apart from the main group, and few of us had the opportunity to learn to get along comfortably together. Now we know how easy it is for people to attach negative expectations and biases to people with different cultures or abilities, particularly when we have only known them at a distance or in stereotypical roles.

The need to belong and have a sense of community is basic for every human being. In a diverse society and world, we no longer live and work in separate enclaves. We all need to know how to function within the larger group and be able to accept our differences. Experience in working out individual and group rights and responsibilities is increasingly important.

Communities and early childhood programs all across the United States now have a mandate to "include." In many instances, inclusiveness represents a deep change in the approach we take toward managing groups, and it changes the basic cultural assumptions with which many of us grew up. When we talk about teaching diverse groups of children and providing the highest quality of services for them, we must take as a starting point our own beliefs about children and families. The mandate of inclusion requires teachers to become responsive to the special needs and abilities of *all* children as individuals. Developing

positive, bias-free beliefs and behaviors in children requires vigilance in *our* behaviors and interactions with
children so as not to perpetuate exclusion practices from
the past. Reflecting on one's own attitudes and responses
as the two teachers do in these stories provides one
means to this end.

**Sherry Holliday** chose to write about inclusiveness
because of her personal experiences in advocating for
diversity and nonbias. She set her sights on a teaching
position in the public school system after she began and
then completed a graduate program in early childhood
special education. **Diane Miller Parker** believes all children
should have the opportunity to learn in a developmentally
appropriate environment. She says her perspective has
been most influenced by her own role in mothering and
her advocacy work for children with special needs.

*—Susan Klein*

# Sherry Holliday

Sherry Holliday

M y earliest memory of special needs was having a first-grade classmate who wore leg braces because he had had polio. I felt some sympathy for him, thinking how sad it must have been for him never to be able to play as the rest of us did. But I was afraid of him too, worrying that I might catch the disease. Also there was a special class, which everyone knew was for the slow learners or dummies. I knew I never wanted to be put in that class.

I remember wanting to be able to share such worries with my mom or dad. But life was hard in rural southern Ohio, and I was the oldest of five children. I was 13 when Mother died of cancer and Dad was forced to split apart our family.

After finishing high school, I left my foster family and was on my own, completing an associate degree in applied science. As part of my studies, I did several practicums that involved learning about and working with adults with severe mental retardation. These experiences were funded by a federal grant for training mental health technicians. Each practicum focused on working in the community in a social services situation.

Some images from those experiences remain crystal clear for me today. One setting at an old, dilapidated building I recall with trepidation. My responsibility was a behavior-modification program with a young woman: teaching her to walk up and down stairs. I used small candies as motivation. She wanted the candies but could not get the message that lifting her leg led to getting candy. When not working with me, my student joined other adults in a large central room —a scene beyond imagination! Some adults were naked or diapered and leashed to a central pole, which they would circle endlessly like May Day dancers. I remember people crying or calling out and one woman holding a doll. Their caretakers stood before a wall-mounted television, watching daytime soap operas and folding endless piles of laundry. I could hardly wait for my practicum there to be over. So my

*Sherry Holliday*, M.S., has been a preschool teacher in a Montessori program, manager of her own horticulture and landscape design business, and a substitute teacher in the public school system. Recently she assumed a co-head teacher position at the Montessori School in Bloomington, Indiana.

first experiences working with adults with severe mental retardation were startling, negative, and even frightening.

A few years later, I learned about the Montessori philosophy of education, though initially I didn't know that Maria Montessori began her work with young children identified as "deficient." From the start I found the Montessori approach appealing. I began work at a Montessori school administered by a Catholic charity service, with support from the United Way. The children, mostly African American and Hispanic, lived in low-income housing projects. Among the staff, there was a spirit of activism. This experience was a satisfying one for me and influenced my decision to seek an undergraduate degree in early childhood education. Our school undoubtedly had children who today would be identified as having learning disabilities. We saw them as "poor and needy" — another label with biases, I now see.

By age 20 I had guardianship of my four siblings, and at 26 I was married and had one sibling still at home. I completed my undergraduate degree in early childhood education at age 30. My training included no information or instruction about children with special needs, but I gave it no thought at the time.

After receiving my degree, I worked at another Montessori program, this time with preschool children from middle-class, college-educated families. After I had taught there for five years, the program enrolled a child with identifiable special needs. He was not assigned to my classroom, but I observed my neighbor teacher's challenges and experiences. She felt the boy enriched the classroom by enabling the other children to learn about his special needs. But as I observed from a distance, I was relieved that the boy was not in my classroom. I guess I was still afraid.

## Moving into special education

Returning after a few years away from teaching, I wanted a challenge beyond working with privileged children in a private preschool. At the suggestion of friends, I thought about a public school position with young children with special needs. Teaching jobs in special education were increasing, but I still had some reluctance and fears.

Exploring options for graduate school, I learned about a special project that offered financial assistance for teachers to go for additional training in early childhood special education. With much ambivalence I entered this program. I soon learned about various syndromes and their characteristics, the history of the Americans with

Disabilities Act, and inclusion and mainstreaming. I met many people working with children with disabilities of various kinds. But all this remained academic until I began working as a substitute teacher in the local schools.

As a substitute I was in dozens of classrooms, most of them kindergarten through sixth grade, and I often served as the special education teacher assisting in the regular classroom or as a special needs teaching assistant. I never would have chosen to be a teaching substitute, but I was told that it was the best way to secure a full-time teaching position.

One day I observed three 4- to 5-year-old girls playing comfortably together. One was a teacher's daughter who had no disabilities; the other two had been labeled as "communication handicapped." The girls themselves seemed unaware of any differences separating them. Seeing their evident ease, I wondered at what age children become aware of or affected by differences in cognitive or functioning abilities.

In the class also was a 5-year-old boy with a breathing problem that required him to come to school with a tank, a long plastic tube attached to a device at his neck, and his own nurse. Despite his mobility problems and lack of speech, he was all over the classroom and into many different activities. When his cord became entangled in toys or chairs the other children were using, they seemed oblivious. His nurse said that most adults see only the problems the disability creates but not what a pleasant, happy child he is.

Another time as inclusion teacher for a third-grade class, I was responsible for teaching a one-hour math lesson to a group of 12 to 15 children with learning difficulties. Two cadet teachers and a student teacher joined me to teach the lesson on adding single digits. In addition to having difficulty with the math aspects, the children were not at all interested in sitting still for an hour, doing table work, waiting for assistance, and staying on task. The "math class from hell," one of the teachers called it. For me it was the beginning of questioning the educational approach I was using rather than assuming the problems were inherent in the children. I thought about whether grouping slow math learners is a good idea. They seemed swamped by each other's frustrations. I also thought that the lengthy lesson and the reliance on worksheets were contributing to the failure of the instruction. In shorter time blocks and with active games or manipulatives, these children would have been more engaged, I thought, and learning more successfully.

More doubts arose when I served as in-school suspension teacher at a middle school. All the children in suspension that day were boys. One had autism and another was so energetic that I worried about how difficult it must be for him to sit through a full day of classes. Was it appropriate to expect him to stay focused in the classroom all day? Perhaps he needed to run laps around the track occasionally! With his pressing need to vent excess energy, he seemed poorly served by a program that could only teach him if he sat still and focused for considerable periods of time.

## Examining my own reactions

Having gotten my feet wet through such experiences, I continue asking myself more and more questions about my own biases and preconceived ideas about children. I wonder how children perceive themselves within the classroom community. When do children begin to be aware of their similarities and differences?

I have heard teachers say that the special education teacher in an inclusion setting may feel like a second-class teacher. Losing her classroom, they say, she loses her autonomy. I don't think about inclusion this way. But maybe if I were in that situation and felt I was perceived as an assistant, I wouldn't feel good about it.

What I have found is that it doesn't matter if I know about a child's diagnosis or label. In the end, what's important is finding out what works for me and that child. I am continuing to examine my own biases and becoming more aware of the language people use when they describe someone or a circumstance. Now when I hear words that seem to carry negative connotations about a child or parent, I speak up. I am conscious of how unaware I was before.

I want to embrace inclusion, although I still cringe when I am introduced to worst-case scenarios. In the graduate course I just completed on management and behavior disorders, we observed and discussed children with behaviors more challenging than I felt I could handle. I still lack confidence when it comes to children with special needs, and I can better relate to parents' fears and concerns than I could in the past.

I am beginning to recognize how I have been affected by my early exposures to disabilities, which were so negative. I'm sure there are many others like me. It helps, I think, to examine where our beliefs, values, and biases come from. Sharing these experiences with others helps too; we recognize ourselves in other people's stories.

Slowly I am getting more comfortable with inclusion. Sometimes it is very challenging, but it is so powerful—and not just for the children with disabilities. All the children gain. I wish my own kids' school had included more children with disabilities. They could have had from the outset a comfort with others' differences that I am still struggling to acquire. To examine my misperceptions and where they come from has taken time and reflection. When we have the opportunity to explore our opinions, the roots of these attitudes may emerge. Though changing one's beliefs doesn't happen overnight, starting to see the source of those feelings is often a turning point in gaining a different perspective.

# Sherry's mentor reflects . . .

As a young child Sherry was aware of the separate classes for those children who looked different or acted differently and who thus were treated differently. Without opportunities to discuss, explore, and clarify her first impressions and perceptions, she naturally drew the conclusion that something was wrong with these children and that they were to be avoided. She reminds us that such childhood experiences and perceptions can create lasting impressions and deep-seated beliefs and attitudes.

To change such beliefs requires delving into their origins in our own lives. And we must consider carefully the early experiences we provide for children, ensuring that these are realistic.

Sherry was introduced to teaching in a Montessori program with a strong sense of community, mutual support, and common mission. In this setting she developed more confidence, commitment, and comfortable feelings about working with children, including those with special needs. Through her substitute teaching in a variety of classrooms, Sherry began to see problems in the special education classes as stemming from curriculum and teaching practices, not inadequacies in the children. Grouping practices, scheduling, and instructional content and method are all involved, she saw, in making good decisions about how to help children grow and learn. Sherry was struck by the risk that a diagnosis or label of a child's special needs may limit our view of her or his capacities. Such labels have their function as a shorthand for identifying crucial characteristics that have legal, educational, and interpersonal significance. But this is only part of what we need to know about the child. Keeping an open mind about what each child is capable of and observing every child closely are among the most important things we can do as teachers.

**T**hink about the first time you encountered someone who struck you as different. How did you and the people around you respond? What was said or implied? What message did you get from this experience?

**T**ry keeping a log of your reactions to children in the classroom as these relate to questions of similarities and differences. How do you support the ideas of *uniqueness* and *difference* in the classroom?

**V**isit a highly inclusive child care program to observe. What do you see in the environment, materials, activities, and teaching strategies that makes inclusion work?

**F**iction that depicts a culture or a lifestyle different from our own or portrays a person with a disability can be eye-opening. A few possibilities you might look for are

*Emily in Love* by S.G. Rubin. 1997. New York: Harcourt Brace.

*Mary Mehan Awake* by J. Armstrong. 1997. New York: Knopf.

*Of Such Small Differences* by J. Greenberg. 1988. New York: Holt & Co.

*Paradise* by T. Morrison. 1997. New York: Knopf.

# Diane Miller Parker

*Now is the time to take possession of my life, to start the impossible, a journey to the limits of my aspirations, for the first time to step toward my loveliest dream. "If I had only known then what I know now" —but now I know enough to begin.*

*—Hugh Prather,* Notes on Love and Courage

When I was 14 years old, my mother volunteered my services at the local Association for Retarded Citizens (ARC). I had never been around people with special needs. I can still remember that first day. I was all dressed up, with nylons! (My mother wanted me to look nice.) What I saw were drooling people with imperfect bodies and unusual behaviors. I felt sick and scared. It took me a week to begin to see them as people, each unique in his or her own way.

Every summer thereafter I worked at the ARC. I had decided that I wanted to teach children with special needs. Making that decision had a dramatic effect on my grades. I had always been an average student, but with a goal in mind I began to get better grades and read more and more.

I graduated with a bachelor's degree in special education, a utopian vision of teaching, and all the answers. With Public Law 94-142 in place, mandating a free and appropriate public education for all school-age children with special needs, jobs were plentiful. I accepted a teaching position in a rural community where children with special needs were bused, some over an hour each way, to a special facility of their own.

I thoroughly enjoyed teaching primary to middle-school children with special needs and was pleased to be part of the instructional staff. At the time I didn't see anything wrong with grouping all the children with special needs in one building. I worked on increasing academic and functional skills in children's deficit areas, depending on how much I believed a child could learn. I taught a skill until the child mastered it 8 out of 10 times. A child would sit at a desk and on my direction point to the color *red*, then name it. I used a lot of behavior

*Diane Miller Parker, M.S., has been a teacher and advocate for children and adults with special needs for a number of years. Currently she teaches in a preschool for children with special needs in Indiana.*

modification and extrinsic reinforcement, such as stickers, chocolate candies, pretzels, small toys, privileges, or a pat on the back, for the right answer or persistent effort.

I never thought about following the child's lead, and I never considered whether the children would be able to generalize the skills they learned to different situations or settings. To foster the skills involved in play, problem solving, or getting along with others never occurred to me. I had been taught — and I believed — that children with special needs needed to be taught in a direct way with systematic external reinforcement. Perhaps I really thought I could "catch them up." Or maybe it was because I saw them as not learning like other children. I thought it was my responsibility to pull them up the instructional ladder. I was teaching splinter skills, fostering dependence, and feeling like I was doing a super job!

The following year I relocated to another school system where I taught 13- to 18-year-olds with moderate mental disabilities. Although my classroom was not in a separate building, it was located in the special education wing. My students were integrated with other students at lunch, but only if they behaved appropriately. They were excluded from eighth-grade or high-school graduation and were not provided a physical education class, so I was told, because no time was available in their schedule.

Although I felt very much a part of the school faculty, my students were treated as separate. As their advocate, I tried to get for them the services, such as physical education, that the other students received. I never thought about asking my colleagues to take some of my children into their classes.

## How differently do children learn?

My daughter was born, and for the next three and a half years I stayed home and learned from my own child. What an experience! I was amazed that my daughter learned without my teaching her. I had studied child development in college, but now I realized I had never really grasped its reality.

I enrolled my child in a preschool program at a local college. I loved the program and the teachers. I saw that she was allowed to choose activities from the sand table, art area, block corner, or other areas. She didn't sit at a table getting structured instruction. There were no worksheets, no external reinforcements. She loved it so much that when a teaching position became available there, I filled in for a while and saw what it was like to teach that way.

Then I joined a school system, working with primary-school children labeled "moderately mentally handicapped," who attended a

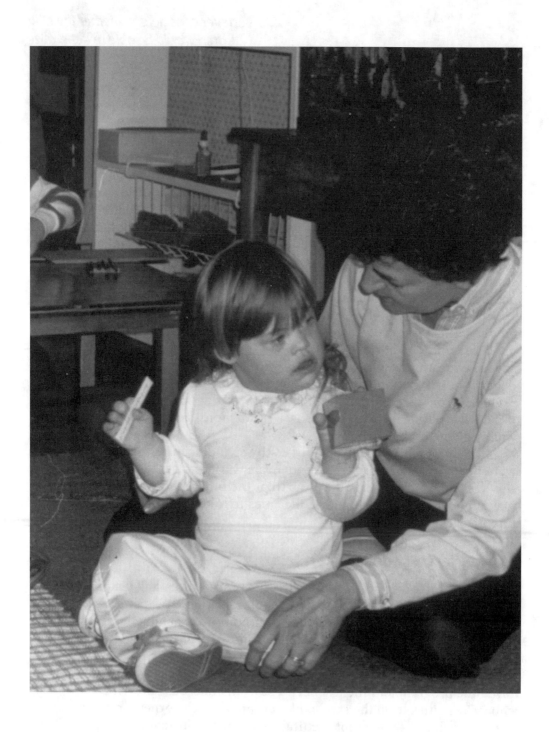

separate center. There was a kindergartner with Down syndrome who I thought would benefit from being in a class enrolling children with fewer disabilities. I was convinced that she was ready for more challenges. When I proposed her transfer, I was called to the principal's office and told that children with Down syndrome belong in the classes for students with moderate mental disability. I could see that I wasn't to leave until I agreed with that recommendation. I agreed to agree because I knew the principal wouldn't listen. That evening at home, however, I called the child's parents and shared my frustration. They decided to pursue what I recommended, and they succeeded.

I began to avoid reading advance information that might bias my thinking about a child. In special education it was common for a child's record to list the name, IQ, mental age, and chronological age. When teachers see a child's IQ of 65 and mental age 2-0, they immediately label him "mildly mentally handicapped" and "functional" as a 2-year-old, before even knowing the child's age. I decided not to start each year that way.

## Looking at children in a new way

After another leave to have two more children, I returned to teach junior-high students who were mildly mentally disabled. Life skills was our focus. Students followed my direction, seemed comfortable with each other, and felt like a family, so much so that some students did not want any involvement in general education classes. I was proud and pleased.

But one weekend when my husband and I took students on a trip to a big city, I saw them in a different way. We ate out, shopped, talked, and swam. But many times my husband gave me a look as if to say, "Why are they doing that?" or "Why can't they do that?" One evening, for example, one of the boys wanted to shower and stayed in the bathroom quite some time. When we knocked and asked if he was OK, he replied that he didn't know how to turn on the shower. The same night a girl put her dress on a hanger, stood in front of the closet, but didn't know where to hang it.

I became painfully aware that my students did not have many of the skills they needed to be independent; instead, they were very dependent on me. In my pursuit of teaching them the right way to do things, I had not allowed them to experience, test and err, and problem solve. I had taught them how to be compliant and fit into a general education program but had been sabotaging their ability to function outside the safety of my classroom. Why did it take me so long to think about all of this? Was it this trip and the presence of another observer, my husband, that got me to see what was happening?

Special education took on new meaning from then on. No longer would I think about it as a *place* —a place where the students didn't have to solve problems, where I didn't set high expectations. I began to think more in terms of equipping them for independence. I also thought about how my own role should fit with the rest of the teaching team.

## Moving toward inclusion

The next year I had the chance to teach the early childhood special education class, and I took it. My choice was influenced by the events of the previous teaching year as well as what I had seen with my own children. I knew that I now wanted a classroom in which children learned as I had observed my own children learning: by active exploration, not being required to sit and learn ABCs or numbers with worksheets or flash cards. I wanted my students to learn by playing, exploring their interests, and solving problems. I wanted them to have opportunities to construct solid understandings through their own experiences and interactions not only with teachers but with peers.

This change in teaching practice wasn't easy and immediate. I had attended some workshops to prepare me for using a constructivist, responsive approach —our school uses a High/Scope approach —but such a major change was a process. With each new experience, I was more convinced how much better it would be if the children with special needs could learn side-by-side with their peers and not always one-on-one for each child.

Although I was working to change my teaching practices in the classroom, I found this way of fostering learning easier at home with my own children. There I didn't have goals to write, nor did I have to answer to anyone or explain my actions. In my classroom I now found myself always thinking, always watching the children's every move, trying to expose them to various experiences. Because it was difficult to convince parents that what I was doing would work and that making choices was beneficial, I was often tempted to switch back to a more direct teaching approach.

In the first year our early childhood special education team began to create linkages with other preschools and child care centers. We rented a room at the local child care center and together we participated in inservice training. We were trying to encourage mainstreaming of our children with special needs into their classrooms of typically developing children. Initially we were able to recruit three children from the center to participate in my classroom, although the children thought of themselves more as "mothers" than as playmates. I also met and spent time with neighborhood family child care providers, hoping to be able to secure some spots in their programs for my young children with special needs.

## Working for inclusive placements

My first experience in helping the parent of a young child with special needs locate child care placement was a learning experience for me. Chris was a 3-year-old with autism. At the child care center Chris's parents had selected, the staff sounded enthusiastic and asked to visit and observe Chris in my classroom. I gave them all kinds of information about autism. I was excited, thinking that they would see what Chris *could* do and how well he interacted with the other children.

The center staff came and observed, but we heard nothing for more than a month. The parents and I were anxious, knowing that the child care opening might not remain available for long. In my call to the child care director, I was told that staff were really busy and hadn't had a chance to talk about Chris. I waited another few days and tried again. This time the director said they were hesitant to start a new child in the next few weeks, with summer break so close at hand. I offered my assistance and support. The director replied that they hadn't said no yet. "We will discuss it more and call you," she concluded.

No calls. I called again and again. Finally, I was told that the staff had concerns based on their observation of Chris in my class. On that day, they reminded me, they saw him climb up on the bookshelf, something he rarely does. They also saw three adults working with 12 children. They refused Chris because they felt he would need one-on-one direction, take teachers' time from other children, and be out of place because he couldn't talk. If the family was willing to pay for an extra staff person, they would reconsider. I was devastated.

I assumed a lot of the responsibility for the rejection of Chris. Perhaps I'd given the child care center too much information about Chris's disability before they met him. Had I been taking too much my classroom?

Chris's parents and I tried another child care program. This time I went with the parents and Chris to the center and intervened in my teacher role only when I felt it necessary. Rather than bombard the director with a lot of information, I let her see Chris in that setting and judge for herself. Chris was accepted and is now enrolled. Although we're all experiencing the roller-coaster ups and downs of his settling in, it seems to be working. As problems arise, the staff deal with them. For example, one day Chris ran out of the center, so they moved him

to a room where he wasn't by the outside door. The staff, the family, and I work together to ensure that Chris's inclusion is successful for everyone. We jointly solve problems that come up. The center's expectations are appropriate for Chris. Instead of seeing his limitations or his perceived need for assistance, they view Chris for what he can do and who he is.

I wonder about my eager efforts with the first center. I was a determined advocate, but I emphasized the condition, not Chris. I framed Chris by his autism, rather than letting the image develop of his just being Chris. This experience makes me wonder about other children who are framed by other labels or conditions. My learning has forced me to think about all the "frames" I put around children — from test scores, labels, and physical conditions to my personal beliefs and individual biases. I am working on leaving each child's image unframed and open to new possibilities and opportunities.

In my own classroom I've watched and listened as children ask questions about children who aren't talking, walking, or interacting as they do. We answer these questions head on. If someone calls a 5-year-old a baby because he doesn't walk or talk and does wear diapers, I say, "Yes, he doesn't walk, talk, or use the bathroom because his muscles aren't working like ours, but he is not a baby." A simple explanation usually works. My classroom's children are learning and experiencing diversity —in this case, differing abilities. But diversity is also there in other less visible ways, and I remind myself to address these areas as well: differences in family and cultural background, attitude, and expectation. Again I work toward not framing or defining children by these differences.

## Looking back and looking forward

I've had to be honest and flexible and look back to see what I could have done differently or what I need to change. It's easy to fall back into old habits, do something a certain way because it is easier or more familiar.

I'm fortunate to be working with early childhood special education staff who aren't afraid of change (maybe we have fears, but we try anyway). Early in my teaching career, I worked alone. As a member of a team, I now realize the value of being able to share different perspectives and backgrounds. We discuss concerns, share information, and try to help each other see situations differently. In addition, we continue to build strong relationships with the early childhood programs in our community.

In my loveliest dream children are treated as *children* first. Now I see that for 25 years I've been on a journey. In my first writing about biases and inclusion, I looked at others and what I perceived as their biases. Then I had to address my own. Looking back over this journey, I didn't realize I was seeing the disability and not the child as a child first. Another bias was thinking of play as a waste of time for children with special needs. Now I work to develop an environment and curriculum that respect the enormous benefits of play and children learning from one another.

As a special educator, I was biased in linking diagnosis with placement. I categorized children and then limited them to predetermined ability levels. A child with autism, for instance, was severely or profoundly disabled. I was biased in thinking that as a specialist *I* had the knowledge that early childhood providers needed before they could enroll a child with special needs. I have been trying to learn how to give up some of the control and empower others to work through problems, each adding his or her own expertise to the solution.

I think many professional special educators have felt we get the necessary understanding and information about a child without conferring with parents —almost wanting not to hear their views of their child. Now I see how important it is to talk with families as well as other teachers and specialists. Reflecting on the old biases, I think that as teachers we think *we know* what children need. And thus we do things our same old way, not really listening to parents, not tuning in to each child's needs. We have to keep all this in mind to find what is the best education for each child.

# Diane's mentor reflects . . .

A special educator by training, Diane describes her early work experience within a self-contained special education class as successful and rewarding—within her framework at the time. She worked hard to increase the children's academic and functional skills by using behavior modification, extrinsic reinforcement, and direct instruction. She saw her role as pulling her children up the instructional ladder, as well as advocating for them when they weren't getting what other children were receiving, such as physical education.

While teaching in this special education classroom and experiencing her own children, Diane began to rethink her teaching role. Changing from the practice we've been taught, she reminds us, is a very personal experience. She also felt the pressure of needing to convince others, including parents, that the changes in her teaching methods would benefit the children with special needs.

Envisioning these children being taught with typically developing peers was an even further stretch in Diane's change process but a step she was able to take, with time and support from colleagues. Her gradual shift began with her welcoming typical children into her special education classroom. Over time Diane became eager to place children with special needs in community settings. Change often comes in stages.

Diane recounts her initial efforts to help Chris move from her classroom into a community child care center. In her distress when he was not accepted, she puzzled over what went wrong and considered her own role, including the extensive information she had shared about autism. Knowing what information to share in such situations is a challenge for us all. In our eagerness to be helpful, we strive to convey a complete picture of the challenges a child presents and may unduly raise others' anxieties and doubts about coping with him. Too often we view a child through the lens of disability and not in his full identity as a developing child.

Diane also muses about issues of ownership and expertise. She now sees the knowledge about a child with a disability as shared among special educators, early childhood educators, and parents. She has journeyed from working alone to becoming a member of a team, and she finds the relationships with other team members have strengthened her resolve to continue to grow and change.

**R**eflect upon some of your own classroom experiences in settings in which there were children with special needs. What responses did you get to your questions about children's different needs?

**T**hink about a previously held idea, value, or belief on which you have changed your thinking. What prompted your change? Was this change supported by others?

**T**ake one personal label you've lived with—something you often have been perceived as being, such as smart, quiet, outgoing, strong-willed. How has this label benefited you? How has it impeded you, pressured you, or limited your possibilities?

**I**f you are currently teaching, ask a colleague to spend some time in your classroom and make observations about the environment, materials, activities, and interactions with respect to reinforcing or combating stereotypes or biases. Together, talk about the strengths and the areas that need to be changed (if you are not teaching, observe a classroom from this same perspective).

## *Resources for further exploration of this topic*

### Books and periodicals

Hoyson, M., B.V. Jamieson, P.S. Strain, & B.J. Smith. 1998. Duck, duck—colors and words: Early childhood inclusion. *Teaching Exceptional Children* (March/April): 66-71.

Jones, H.A., & M.J. Rapport. 1997. Research-to-practice in inclusive early childhood education. *Teaching Exceptional Children* (November/December): 57-62.

Paasche, C.L., L. Gorril, & B. Strom. 1990. *Children with special needs in early childhood settings.* Reading, MA: Addison-Wesley-Longman.

Prather, H. 1977. *Notes on love and courage.* Garden City, NY: Doubleday.

U.S. Department of Health and Human Services, Administration for Children and Families, Administration on Children, Youth and Families, Child Care Bureau. 1997. *Passages to inclusion: Creating systems of care for* all *children.* Monograph for state, territorial, and tribal child care administrators. Washington, DC: National Child Care Information Center.

*Young Exceptional Children,* a peer-reviewed publication of the Division for Early Childhood (DEC) of the Council for Exceptional Children (CEC), 1920 Association Drive, Reston, VA 22091.

### Videotapes

*A circle of inclusion.* 1993. Produced by Raintree Montessori School with the University of Kansas. 27 min. Lawrence, KS: Learner Managed Designs (800-467-1644).

*Inclusion.* 1994. Parts 1 & 2. 33 min. New York: Insight Media (212-721-6316).

*Everybody's schoolhouse.* 1994. 15 min. New York: Insight Media.

*Playing together: Cooperating together.* 1993. Produced by the University of Missouri —Columbia. 46 min. Lawrence, KS: Learner Managed Designs.

### Websites

Association for the Care of Children's Health —http://www.look.net/acch

Division of Early Childhood of the Council for Exceptional Children— www.soe.uwm.edu/dec/dec.html

Frank Porter Graham Child Development Center/The University of North Carolina at Chapel Hill —http://www.fpg.unc.edu

National Early Childhood Technical Assistance System (NEC*TAS)—http:// www.nectas.unc.edu

### Community contacts

Consult your local early intervention or public school system for information and workshops.

# Emergent Curriculum 5

**Brenda Julovich and Tracy Heyob**
*with Darcee Hume-Thoren as mentor*

Naturally curriculum is a common topic of discussion among teachers. Bits and pieces of information and questions regarding curriculum are bounced about whenever teachers get together:

I have an art project you might want to use when you do dinosaurs.

We're doing some really interesting things right now; the children are so excited about building since the bank construction down the block began last week.

I need some songs about the farm. Does anybody know of a few good ones?

I have some great stories planned for the holidays, but the children haven't been very attentive lately. We'll see how it goes.

Such exchanges reveal a great deal about the day-to-day events in these programs, but they often float along on the surface of real curriculum issues. Prepared curricula that come from standard text materials or from each teacher's files may provide a sense of security. However, we must ask ourselves, "Are the answers to children's curricular needs so clear-cut, so predictable?" Theorists emphasize that children's knowledge is not directly transferred to children. It is built through the child's own efforts to make meaning out of her concerns, activities, and experiences. This view suggests that shaping the curriculum should be a constant process of planning, evaluating, reflecting, and planning once again. In other words, curriculum should be personalized and ever changing.

Thus an emergent curriculum responds to, expands, and builds upon the ideas and interests of the children in the group, collectively and individually. Of course teachers have expectations about the skills and knowledge that are important for children to develop, and these are always part of their planning process. Then by observing and interacting with children, teachers develop the materials, resources, and opportunities to foster the learning of the unique individuals in their care.

One strength of an emergent curriculum is that it is based on the real-life connections children make as they explore and react to the world around them. This process of exploration, investigation, and creation—where it goes and how it looks—results from the negotiating that occurs between teacher and children and between children as well. Such a relationship of give-and-take shapes the emergent curriculum and sustains a dynamic learning process for teachers and learners.

The following journals represent the journeys of two teachers engaging in this give-and-take while striving to develop more responsive, child-sensitive curricula. **Brenda Julovich**'s efforts to include children with special needs led her to a new realization of the unique needs of all children and how emergent curriculum responds to those needs. **Tracey Heyob** chose to reflect on emergent curriculum because she believes that in teaching there is always something changing to think about. Every encounter with children may bring new discoveries about each of the children and about the art of teaching.

—Darcee Hume-Thoren

# Brenda Julovich

Brenda Julovich

A few years ago, as a recent graduate, I was substituting in the schools with the hope of getting a permanent teaching job. I often subbed for the music teacher at an elementary school, and it was there I had my first experience in teaching children with special needs. Never in any school setting, as a child or young-adult student, had I been involved in interacting with a child with special needs. As the substitute music teacher in this K–2 building, I now taught a 25-minute-period class of children whose disabilities were labeled "severe and profound."

There was no way to escape my feelings of discomfort with being responsible for this class. I had no experience to help me know what I should or could do with these children. I felt unqualified to teach music on my own to children with special needs.

On my days substituting in that school, I often used my teacher's break to visit another special education classroom, trying to learn something that would make me feel less anxious. I was eager to gain some experience that would enable me to teach these children with more comfort and success.

The next fall I was hired to teach first grade at the school where I had substituted. My biggest job was to provide experiences to help my children read. I read stories aloud. We had a silent reading period every day. The children checked out books from the library for our own library corner in the room. We wrote experience stories as a group. Children dictated stories that I typed, and they later made these into books. Using invented spelling at first, they wrote their own stories and letters. They also read stories to each other.

Mostly, however, the children met with me in ability groups and used a basal series provided by the school. Forming the basis of my reading instruction, this series provided me with an organization of skills to be taught, controlled vocabulary, workbooks, enrichment sheets, unit and level tests for documentation, and stories for a variety of reading abilities. At the time I was grateful for the framework and structure this reading series provided during this year when everything I did was a first and much was brand new. To my inexperienced eyes this curriculum looked as if it worked for everyone.

*Brenda Julovich, M.S., has been a first-grade teacher in Bloomington, Indiana, for the past 12 years.*

## But he doesn't fit . . .

"Edward's mother is really pushing hard to get him into a reading group with first graders," the special education teacher told me. "Do you think you have a reading group he could join?"

Why did a special educator think I had something to offer Edward? He was mildly to moderately disabled with Down syndrome. I knew nothing about teaching a child with special needs to read, and surely his mother was being unrealistic! I thought, "How could he learn to read in a classroom set up for typically developing children with a teacher who does not have the knowledge to help him?"

After the initial arrangements were made for Edward to come to my classroom, I found it hard to relate to the excited communications from his mother. She was so sure he would learn more if he sat with the other children, with the same book they had in their hands. She was emphatic about her son seeing examples of other children reading. I couldn't see how that would matter. I worried about *my* abilities to instruct Edward. Teaching him was my responsibility, not the children's.

Edward came on the first day, virtually swaggering in with the "real" reading book in his hand. He was obviously proud and excited to be in our class and in a reading group, which perhaps gave him a new sense of belonging. He was primed to "behave and pay attention," and at first he did. He held his book and followed the words as pairs

or groups of children read the simple sentences on each page. Next we spent some time talking about the vocabulary and phonics skills and then reviewed the instructions for the workbook pages. This was a daily routine.

Several weeks later I had reached the limits of my patience. Edward wasn't keeping up with the group. He couldn't behave. He was not motivated to sit at the reading table. His book no longer thrilled him, and I had to admit that reading about Ken and Sarah at the park was pretty dull. In truth, I really didn't know how to teach reading any differently. The other children weren't misbehaving like Edward, so I thought it couldn't be the books or my methods. What I didn't realize was that the other children simply were more able to tolerate the boredom and mask their frustration with the dry basal reader. The situation disintegrated, and I chalked up the inclusion of Edward as an effort that was worth the try but just didn't work.

Edward's mother called the school and asked to speak to me early one morning before the children arrived. She was obviously disappointed that Edward was no longer having reading in my room. I wished I didn't have to say what I knew would be hard for her to hear, but even my limited experience had taught me it was best to be straightforward. She was frustrated that communication about his reading assignments had not been more frequent. Although she had a point, the biggest issue was that Edward wasn't learning like the other children. I believed I couldn't be the one to help him.

Since it was decided that Edward would no longer come to my room for reading, he would remain in his self-contained classroom. I concluded that I didn't have the skills or the ability to give Edward the personal attention he needed. I felt overwhelmed by what had been asked of me, and I didn't know how to handle the situation differently.

## Seeing through the eyes of a parent

That summer, I had a conversation with my friend Joanne that gave me a lot to think about. "Do you know anything about the rules and regulations that go with special education?" she asked. Her daughter Annie has Williams syndrome, a genetic disorder causing mental retardation. "Annie is going to have a case conference, and the evaluation team will be talking about her placement in the public schools. I want her to be with the kindergartners, but I'm not sure if the school will do that." Joanne and her husband were desperate for information about Annie's options and what they could legally request.

"I just want her to be with the other kids!" Joanne explained. Fresh from my experience with Edward, I asked, "Why wouldn't you want

Annie in a special education classroom? Why would you want her in the regular kindergarten rather than in a self-contained class where she could get more individualized attention?" Joanne answered, "I want her to go to the neighborhood school with her brother. I want Annie to have conversations and to be around children talking and playing with one another. I want her to see that other children don't lie down on the floor and have tantrums. She may not learn to read as early as the others, but I want her to be exposed to children enjoying books." Joanne's response was so heartfelt and sure.

As a member of the team working to help Annie learn, Joanne asked for an aide to accompany Annie to kindergarten. Fortunately the kindergarten teacher was open to the idea of including Annie. The plan was that Annie would spend the mornings in a self-contained special education classroom. At first she would attend kindergarten in the afternoon for one hour, and this time would lengthen gradually until she was fully included in the kindergarten for the entire afternoon. This worked out well, and the following year Annie was fully included in a first-grade class. I followed this collaborative process closely, with boundless admiration for those involved.

As I was keeping up with Annie's progress and learning about the perspective of her family, I began to be more aware of a boy named Chad at my school. As Joanne reminded me of the value of Annie being with children in a regular classroom and described the adaptations of materials and curriculum in Annie's room, I watched Chad use his eye-gaze charts and light talker to communicate to his speech teacher. He would be coming to first grade soon—wheelchair, computer, chin switch, eye-gaze charts, communication boards, aide, and all.

That next year Chad moved to the first-grade classroom next to my mine. The teacher seemed to deal easily with the many challenges she faced. I thought, "Perhaps it was just a matter of getting to know the child, just as we need to get to know any child who comes into our class." I heard that Chad would continue in the first grade another year, but I didn't think about this in relation to myself. I was busy with my own class and with thoughts of a summer with my family, which now included a 15-month-old son.

Having a child of my own had provided insights into my teaching. I examined further the most basic of parents' expectations: Shouldn't any child in a classroom be treated with the utmost care and respect for his individuality, regardless of abilities or disabilities? Should any child be denied access to an environment that allows for learning and socializing with her peers? Should any child be denied a sense of belonging? I was beginning to understand more fully why some parents were pushing for access to regular classrooms. As a parent now, I knew I would.

## Learning through firsthand experience

*"I want Annie to have conversations and to be around children talking and playing with one another. I want her to see that other children don't lie down on the floor and have tantrums . . . . I want her to be exposed to children enjoying books."*

I now saw the importance of inclusion, but that didn't remove the discomfort of doing it in my classroom. When I came back in the fall, I received my class list for the year. There was Chad's name on the list. I walked into the principal's office and said to him, "Please, I just have to say this one time, and then I'll do the best job I can: Good grief — look who's on my list!"

The principal laughed. He understood my need to share with someone how nervous I was about doing the right thing for this child. I resolved to make it a positive situation, but I had no inkling of the things I would learn from this child or the influence he would have on my teaching for many years to come.

The first few weeks in my classroom with Chad and his aide Heather were spent simply in figuring out how to help Chad *be* in school. Most of our time was spent learning how to communicate with Chad. He was usually very patient, considering the large number of people he dealt with every day. We all had to learn to ask yes/no questions and how to use the eye-gaze chart. (An eye-gaze chart attaches to the child's wheelchair and allows for pictures to be clipped onto it. A child who cannot speak or point directs his gaze at a particular picture to demonstrate a preference. For example, at choice time, pictures of the activity areas are displayed so the child can indicate the area he would like to go to by gazing at it.)

We also had to figure out a physical arrangement in the classroom that would accommodate Chad's chair and computer. Scheduling Heather's lunch break and the variety of necessary therapies for Chad also required planning and flexibility. For a while it was a daily process of smoothing out kinks and solving a wide variety of small problems as they arose.

Within the first few weeks, I was developing close relationships with the children, just as they were with each other. It was sobering to realize that this same development was not occurring with Chad. As I thought about this, I realized the difference—Chad was not as free to come to me if he had a question or an idea. His interactions were not nearly as frequent or spontaneous as those of the other children. Chad usually directed his questions or comments to Heather, who had great insight into what he was saying and how he learned. I was not nearly as adept.

### Depending on one another in the classroom

The breakthrough day was one of the nuttiest of the year but a day that forged a new relationship. Heather had called in sick, and there was no substitute available because the bad weather meant many absent staff throughout the system. I remember the chaos as I began removing Chad's winter coat, boots, mittens, hat, and scarf at the same time I was trying to greet the other children, listen to their comments, and answer their questions. So I started doling out jobs: "Here, you hang this strap up and get his backpack." Pointing to someone else, I continued, "You get this strap to his seat, and I'll get this one. Now, let's see, you get his communication board out of the backpack, and someone else, please find his shoes."

It was the first of many times that I would see the children help in the classroom and show caring far beyond what I had seen in the past. And they weren't just doing it for me. They were eager to help Chad, even though they understood it meant waiting to have their own needs met.

With Chad situated for the time being, we all met in a large group for the opening of the day. This was the usual procedure in which we took attendance, determined our lunch count, and sized up the daily activities. We talked about what the children wanted to write about in their journals and about some other activities they would be doing. During reading, Chad stayed by me and met with each of the reading groups. This was different from his usual participation, but he enjoyed being exposed to all the stories the various groups were reading, even when the stories were above his reading level. This was a reminder to me that children can have very meaningful experiences with literature that has been judged too difficult for them to read. By sharing the pictures, the personalities, and the stories, children realize the joy of reading.

Being in this new situation — on my own with Chad — took effort on both our parts. I had to change gears and ask yes/no questions instead of the open-ended ones I usually posed. I began to notice variations in Chad's posture, his head position, and his eyes. These things were all part of his communication, just as they are a part of anyone else's nonverbal communication. We all had to learn Chad's system; he knew it well. Patiently and effectively, he taught me and the other staff to communicate with him.

## Making learning meaningful

My fears lessened as I learned more about Chad. I could see how capable he was, and the task of teaching him to read didn't seem quite so overwhelming. My task became one of setting priorities: What were the most valuable learning experiences for Chad? Because Chad often needed twice the usual amount of time to complete an activity, I wanted to make certain his experiences were meaningful and productive; I didn't want to waste precious moments on things that weren't valuable or didn't work for us.

I wanted him to have a writing experience every day. The first writing he did was with his computer's new word processing program. Using the chin switch to pick letters as they were scanned took a great deal of practice and effort. This made me very aware that he should choose what he wanted to write about. Otherwise, it wasn't worth it to him to put so much concentration and effort into the task. This realization made me think about the daily reading and writing activities of all the children and how to make them more meaningful to each child.

One day we were using the usual oral question-and-answer routine to try to understand what Chad wanted to say, but to no avail. Heather had no way of helping him start, but he was clearly eager to convey something to us. On his own he began the slow scanning that generated letters on his screen, and we sat watching in suspense. Slowly the words appeared: "JB IS LOD."

At first we were puzzled. But remembering that in his group home he shared a room with a boy named J.B., I shouted, "J.B. is loud!" Chad squealed and nearly catapulted out of his chair, thrilled that I understood what he was trying to say. In our elation we roamed the halls with Chad, looking for anyone who wanted to read the sentence he had written. As each person said something like "Yes, J.B. is loud, isn't he?" Chad was thrilled all over again.

Chad experienced a new power in his daily efforts to tell what he knew or thought. From then on, he wrote every day about topics of his choice. He communicated ideas that were difficult or impossible for him to express any other way. Using the computer he expressed feelings, described past events, shared his wishes, made a Christmas list. I gained a deeper understanding of the relationship between a child's personal use of language and the process of learning to read.

Chad met with his reading group whenever the children gathered at the reading table. I wanted him to feel that he was a part of the discussions with his peers. Chad vocalized the words as best he could when he read aloud in a small group. The new basal reader series we were using was more meaningful and engaging to the children than the one we had been using when Edward was with us. When we read the play *The Three Little Pigs,* Chad played a very convincing wolf. With great expression he huffed and puffed, causing such hilarity that the whole class stopped working to pay attention.

## Setting priorities

There wasn't enough time, I was finding, for Chad to do workbook pages *and* to write in his journal. Using the computer to write his own words, thoughts, and feelings was so much more engrossing than doing workbook pages. Carefully considering Chad's interests and what he had time to accomplish, I moved workbook pages down on the priority list. As the need to make good use of our time with Chad forced me to weed out less meaningful activities, I began to ask myself, "Isn't every child's time just as valuable as Chad's? Shouldn't I be prioritizing all the children's activities in the same way?"

## Everybody learning, everybody teaching

Currently I have in my class a boy, Bobbie, who suffered a traumatic brain injury in a car accident a year ago. In the classroom he works at a desk clustered with others to form a group. Now I recognize how much all children benefit from peer collaboration and the help they receive from and give to others. As the teacher, I am responsible for the children's learning, but I don't underestimate the extent to which everybody learns and everybody teaches in an emergent curriculum. I remember Edward and think about how he could have benefited from this kind of classroom. Rather than trying to squelch the children's social nature, I now capitalize on it to promote their learning.

While I am still using the basal reading series and, yes, the workbooks, we will soon adopt a new reading curriculum that supports reading and writing in more meaningful ways. I may get the option of taking the money allotted for a new reading series and spending it for trade books, which I could select based on my children's various interests and needs. Though this approach would be more work, it would let many more decisions about the curriculum rest with me. I could make decisions based on my observations of the children rather than a distant publisher's guess as to what stories might interest them.

Already I have altered the way I use the basal series so that Bobbie can participate. For a while I had used the books as they were intended, which put Bobbie in a group by himself based on his reading level and inability to keep pace with the others. He didn't feel good about this, nor did I or the other children. Some children asked rather incredulously, "Are you going to put him in a group all by himself?" Then I thought about the kind of message I was sending to everyone, and that was the end of that. Now Bobbie hears the stories and adds what he can to the group, whether it's chiming in on familiar parts of the story or adding sound effects. He doesn't know all the words, but he is thrilled to be able to contribute.

I look forward to the day when my reading program and the rest of the curriculum provide a variety of meaningful activities and children working together form small groups on the basis of interests and other considerations rather than "ability grouping." I have learned to focus on children's individual interests and take advantage of their social nature to encourage learning. In the years to come, I look forward to exploring these issues more fully. I'm sure that more "young teachers" will come into my classroom and help me learn and develop my skills, just as Edward, Chad, Bobbie, and others have.

# Brenda's mentor reflects . . .

Prepared reading materials provide security and support that first-year teachers often crave. With a preset reading program, however, there is little opportunity to respond to the unique and ever-changing characteristics of the individuals in a classroom. Brenda's journals contrast her early use of prepared curricula with her growing concern for meeting children as individuals.

Brenda moves toward emergent curriculum in her desire to allow for individual interests and learning styles and make the process of learning to read and write more meaningful and engaging for children. Her integration of oral language, reading, writing, and listening rather than on isolated skills gives the children the opportunity to experiment with language use, internalize concepts about how language works, and learn to actively and effectively use language in a variety of ways within a social environment.

Fully recognizing that all children are individuals is an important step toward supporting their learning. Certainly, being informed and equipped with resources is crucial when working with children who have special needs. But the ways we have of categorizing children (e.g., "he has Down syndrome" or "she is shy") can get in the way of our knowing the individual child. Overemphasizing such labels, we form expectations that may end up severely limiting the child's development. To support the individual child's development, we must be alert to her cues and keep an open mind about how much she can progress and in what ways.

A classroom environment in which children accept and appreciate each other as individuals, in which they feel a sense of community and caring for one another—this is what the teacher strives for. Such an environment promotes a free flow of ideas, opinions, and positive interactions. Children are investigators, creators, negotiators, and protagonists. Brenda felt her classroom begin to blossom when the children became aware of their interdependence and their ability—indeed, their responsibility—to help others in the classroom.

She also sees the relationship of emergent curriculum to the kind of inclusive, supportive environment she seeks to create. Through emergent curriculum, teachers model the accepting and valuing of individual differences. Promoting children's acceptance of one another is a goal most teachers consider important. Yet some aspects of our own teaching practice may not reflect real acceptance of children's differences.

By honestly acknowledging the differences in children's interests and abilities, Brenda begins to act on her belief that all children are to be valued and respected. When we divide a group of children by perceived or assessed abilities in narrowly defined academic areas, we validate only a narrow range of skills and the children who have them. We ignore the strengths and potential contributions of many individuals.

As Judith Schickedanz states in *More Than the ABCs: The Early Stages of Reading and Writing,* "When children, and not teaching children, are the focus, meaningful learning takes place" (1986, 125; rev. ed. forthcoming). Teachers must observe and ask questions, find out the child's intentions in terms of what he wants to say or produce, and then provide the materials he needs to express himself—resource books, writing materials, the computer or typewriter, and so on. Giving children opportunities to express what is important to them makes language activities more meaningful. Brenda was struck by this when she saw the enthusiasm and joy generated by Chad's basic act of communication—"J.B. is loud"—and how it enabled him to connect with others.

Think about an interest you had as a young child (a hobby, sport, or special topic). How did you learn about it? How did adults support your learning? Did they select and adapt materials or experiences to meet your needs?

Think about circumstances that make you feel uncomfortable in the classroom—a child, interaction, or event. Why are you uncomfortable? What might you do to gain more information to lessen your anxieties?

When you think about curriculum and how it is determined, what images or mental pictures come to mind? Are these images consistent with the curriculum in your classroom? Create a symbol or representation that reflects your image of curriculum.

Discuss with a friend or colleague your goals for the young children in your setting. Do you have the same goals for all children? What are your highest priority goals for the children? In what ways is your curriculum consistent—or not—with these goals?

.. 

# Tracy Heyob

Tracy Heyob

L ast year I taught a kindergarten class in a pre-K center. I thought I had created a well-run, child-sensitive classroom environment. Yet I always went home feeling exhausted and frustrated, as if I were returning from battle. If I felt that way, the children probably did as well. I decided to brainstorm ideas to alleviate the problem. But what was the problem? What was I doing that needed to be done differently?

I had always believed that the key to a successful classroom was setting up an environment and then choosing a theme that would engage children's interest. I listened to the children's conversations to try to determine their interests. I wanted to motivate every child by choosing just the right theme and following through with related activities. But even from the beginning I saw I was not addressing the interests of all the children.

## Letting children decide

When I began to examine the curriculum and what went on in the classroom, I realized that the strongest, most active periods of learning were the times I allowed the children to plan and carry out their own ideas, their own projects. I began to consider how to create more opportunities for the children to pursue their interests and to share and expand those interests through interactions with me and the other children.

How could I be certain a theme or project interested the children? How could I encourage the children to take ownership of the learning process? After some thought I decided to let the children choose the theme. By doing this I could be sure the topic was interesting to the majority of the children, and I would be allowing them to take hold of the decisionmaking process. During group time, we brainstormed and listed ideas for the theme. The children voted on which theme ideas interested them most.

Still I had misgivings about how things in the classroom were going. Although the children's theme selection brought us closer to

*Tracy Heyob*, B.A., has taught young children in a variety of settings. Currently she is a kindergarten teacher at the Meridian Academy of the Arts, a private school in Greenwood, Indiana.

what I envisioned, I could see that the ocean life theme still did not interest everyone. What about those children who voted for another theme? Also, I could see that different aspects of the theme interested different children.

"Where do I go from here?" I thought. I had so many questions that needed to be answered — so many interrelated issues to address. Many of my questions brought me back to the foundation of my work: child development and appropriate practice. What can children do?

What can I do to give them the most engaging and productive learning experiences they could have?

The interests of the children were so varied that, inevitably, by choosing one theme I shut off the investigation of various other topics children wanted to explore. How could I search out the interests of more children? I decided to address the problem by allowing more than one theme. Could I manage more than one focus at a time? Would this allow for meaningful learning on the part of the children and effective facilitation on my part?

There was only one way to find out. I would have the children choose their themes during small-group time. Each small group would determine what direction its project would take. The children chose their theme and then met various times during the week. The first theme-project topics were superheroes, dogs and cats, rocks, and ships.

Before implementing this new approach, I decided to discuss it with my director. She was supportive but also provided a touch of realism. "This sounds wonderful, but it will certainly be a great deal of work for you." I assured her that I was up to the challenge. She encouraged me by providing an article on the project approach that she had found interesting and thought might provide some insights.

## First steps

The project article fascinated me. It was the first I had read about the project approach in relation to emergent curriculum. Seeing that others were headed down the same path, I hoped their experiences could benefit me. I wanted to know how others found time to meet with several small groups every day. I wondered when and how they could collect and organize all the resources and materials each group needed to fully explore their chosen topic.

With these questions unanswered, we began our group projects. I quickly realized that it was virtually impossible for me to meet with each of the four groups on a daily basis. When at first I did attempt to meet with them daily, it was during our free-choice time. The small-group meetings were often interrupted by situations arising with other children, who were participating in free-choice activities. I could give neither set of children, those in the small group or those in free choice, the time and attention they deserved.

What could be done? I decided to meet with only one group each day during free-choice time rather than with all four groups. I believed this might permit me to address the specific small-group needs while still filling the various roles I need to play during free-choice time. The small groups needed me, I was convinced, to provide structure to the discussion, provoke questions, further the development of their ideas, provide materials, and model skills or techniques.

This approach had some advantages, but now I faced a new problem. Meeting with one small group a day meant each group met only once a week! The projects had no opportunity to gain momentum, and the children had lost interest by the time their second small group meeting occurred. I tried to wrap up the projects quickly and helped the children in their efforts to present their projects to the rest of the children. Although the process had been far from ideal, I was encouraged by the children's presentations and discussion surrounding the various projects.

The members of the Superheroes group each chose a favorite character and shared with the other children why they liked that character. The Dogs/Cats group made a poster comparing the two animals. The Rocks group collected a variety of rocks, labeled them, and presented findings in the form of a Rock Museum. The Ships group never got around to sharing its project with the rest of the class—interest in the project was waning. Overall I was encouraged, but I knew how much more meaningful the projects would have been if the children had received more guided time and opportunity to pursue their work in greater depth.

About this time, as part of my participation in the Best Practices project, I began to explore the Reggio Emilia approach and how it related to what I was doing in my classroom. I read *The Hundred Languages of Children: The Reggio Emilia Approach to Early Childhood Education* [see the new edition—Edwards, Gandini, & Forman 1998], which provides insight into the program's history, philosophy, curriculum, and methods, and I watched two videos filmed in Reggio schools. I saw clearly that the way project work occurs in the Reggio Emilia approach is much more natural and less teacher-managed than the way I had been trying to do projects. By overstructuring the process, I was limiting the directions in which the children's explorations could proceed. And perhaps I was thinking too much in terms of themes rather than projects. I knew that I wanted to allow the children's thinking and working together to follow its course rather than controlling it myself. But how could I achieve this?

### Following the children's interests

We had been given an ant farm, and the children had been observing the ants making tunnels. When I asked them, "What could we do with these empty boxes?" they were inspired to make an ant tunnel they could crawl through. Using two large boxes, they made a tunnel,

took it to the playground, and covered it with sand. They crawled through the tunnel, imagining what it must feel like to be an ant. Other enterprises relating to the ants were also developing. The children drew and painted pictures of the ants. We read books about ants, and the children wrote stories about them. Individually and in small groups, the children recorded their observations of the ant farm. We even made ant costumes, and the children got involved in dramatic play about ant life.

Through all this activity I helped when needed and tried to keep ongoing documentation of the development of the project through writing and taking pictures. The children also made a project display. At times, I asked the children questions about their activities and encouraged them to investigate further.

*The children had been observing the ants making tunnels. When I asked them, "What could we do with these empty boxes?" they were inspired to make an ant tunnel they could crawl through.*

During this entire project, there were no structured meeting times. The children chose when and how they would participate. They shared their interests and were exposed to the various interests of the other children. With great excitement, they joined forces to investigate and explore this fascinating topic they had discovered.

The next project began to emerge during a discussion about the coming of spring. Eager for spring, the children were thinking about changes that would be occurring soon. They discussed the warming weather and the activities that nice weather would allow. One child mentioned the summer fair, and the others joined in. Then someone asked if we could have a fair. "Yes!" they all cried. My first thought was, "No, we can't!" I really didn't think that a project of that magnitude was feasible. But before replying I let them discuss and explore the possibilities. What kind of fair? What games, rides, foods, and so on would the fair have? We wrote down all the ideas the children generated. Next we began to think together how we could create these various elements in a Spring Fair of our own.

The children's ideas were so creative! The games they decided to have at the fair were Hit the Cans, Basketball Shoot, Clown Game (throw the ball through a hole in the clown's mouth), Bag Race, and a Running Race. They worked out how they would get the necessary materials for the games. Next they determined what rides should be at the fair. The children decided on a Merry-Go-Round (on the tire swing), Roller Coaster (wagons on the bike path), and Slide Ride (making a tunnel over the slide and then riding down the slide on pillowcases).

Some children volunteered to perform at the fair, so it was decided that a stage would be created. The children also wanted food at their fair—everything from hot dogs to apple pie was named. When I asked them how we could provide those things, their answer was a unanimous "Mommy and Dad!" I reminded them that the fair was theirs and asked how *they* might be able to provide food. One child suggested making cookies and serving lemonade, and we decided to do that.

With only one week to go until the Spring Fair, the children were extremely excited and working very hard. They decided to make a map to show people where the rides and games were, give the location of the stage and show times, and note where the foods were.

Seeing the children working hard, exploring options, and solving problems, I was delighted. Investigating emergent curriculum and the project approach and trying different ways of doing things had transformed our classroom. There's more for me to learn, but I'm on my way!

# Tracy's mentor reflects ...

With increasing awareness of how much children's active engagement enhances their learning, Tracy explored in our mentoring discussions the roles she might play to foster and support child-initiated activities. She played many roles, from observer, problem solver, and participant to provocateur, role model, and instructor. Tracy saw how vital she was to extending and supporting children's ideas and interests. She applied her creative problem solving to figuring out how to make herself available on an equitable basis to support the children's efforts.

Through her reflective practice Tracy learned the value of fellow professionals as a resource. By building a web of professional support, she was able to share ideas, experiences, and information with others. Collaboration also provided valuable insights and perspectives by bringing together individuals from different positions within the same field and from related fields of work. Tracy actively sought answers by exploring the many ways teachers build upon young children's natural enthusiasm for learning and focus on the specific interests of the individual child. In addition to insights from other professionals, she used as resources books, videos, magazines, and journal articles.

In our dialogues Tracy acknowledged the challenge she and all teachers face: the impossibility of being available to all children at all times. Teachers must work at focusing their energies where and when they are needed. She recognized too that for children to investigate a topic and pursue answers and solutions, they must have the time to build connections, reflect on new experiences, and represent their discoveries in a variety of ways. Time is also important in building collaborative relationships between the children and between the children and their teachers.

Through training sessions and the mentoring process, Tracy began to realize that dictating, step by step, what children will do and how they will do it was unnecessary and undesirable. Yet she saw she had other active roles to play. She guided and supported children throughout the learning process by listening and observing, questioning, recording, assisting with or modeling skills and techniques, providing materials and resources, and offering problems for the children to solve.

Through her writing Tracy shows us that learning a way that allows individuals and the group as a whole to progress involves creativity and flexible management skills. She experimented with more and less rigid mechanisms for meeting with children, identifying the sources of the curriculum as it emerged, and assisting children to pursue their interests in individual as well as collective ways.

What are your most vivid memories of experiences in which you were deeply engaged and learning a lot? What were the setting and context for this learning like? How were your feelings in this setting different from your feelings in less-productive, engaging contexts?

Think about the spaces or activities in your classroom where the most interesting children's conversations and questions develop. What characteristics of this context seem to encourage children's interchanges? How can you integrate these qualities into other learning areas or activities?

Recall a specific interaction in which you tried to promote a child's learning. Write down your exchange. Make a list of other ways you might have chosen to interact in this situation. Try keeping an ongoing list of roles or interactions you might employ in the future. Meet with other colleagues to share and discuss ideas and expand your list.

Add a new assessment or documentation process to your everyday classroom life (e.g., observations, interviews with children, conduction-structure assessments, videotaping). Once you find what works for you, explore ways to incorporate the discoveries into your planning process.

## References and other resources for further exploration of this topic

### Books and periodicals

Blasi, M.J., & L. Priestly. 1998. A child with severe hearing loss joins our learning community. *Young Children* 53 (2): 44-49.

Edwards, C., L. Gandini, & G. Forman, eds. 1998. *The hundred languages of children: The Reggio Emilia approach to early childhood education —Advanced reflections.* Norwood, NJ: Ablex.

Goleman, D., P. Kaugman, & M. Ray. 1992. *The creative spirit.* (Companion volume to the videotape below.) New York: Dutton.

Greenwald, C., & J. Hand. 1997. The project approach in inclusive preschool classrooms. *Dimensions of Early Childhood* 25 (4): 35-39.

Helm, J.H., S. Beneke, & K. Steinheimer. 1998. *Teacher materials for documenting young children's work: Using "Windows on Learning."* New York: Teachers College Press. (Available from NAEYC.)

Helm, J.H., S. Beneke, & K. Steinheimer. 1998. *Windows on learning: Documenting young children's work.* New York: Teachers College Press. (Available from NAEYC.)

Jones, E., & J. Nimmo. 1994. *Emergent curriculum.* Washington, DC: NAEYC.

Malaguzzi, L. 1993. For an education based on relationships. *Young Children* 49 (1): 9-12.

Malaguzzi, L. 1994. Your image of the child: Where teaching begins. *Child Care Information Exchange* 96 (March/April): 52-61.

Schickedanz, J.A. 1986. *More than the ABCs: The early stages of reading and writing.* Washington, DC: NAEYC.

### Videotapes

*The creative spirit.* 1992. Produced by PBS. (Reggio Emilia segment, Part 2.) Los Angeles: PBS (Video Division, 4401 Sunset Blvd., Los Angeles, CA 90027).

*To make a portrait of a lion.* 1987. 30 min. Comune di Reggio Emilia, Italy: Centro Documentazione Ricerca Educativa Nidi e Scuole dell'Infanzia (available through Baja Rankin, 346 Washington St., Cambridge, MA 02139).

### Websites

Early Childhood News: The Journal of Professional Development —http://www.earlychildhoodnews.com/explore.htm

ERIC Clearinghouse on Elementary and Early Childhood Education/Reggio Emilia —http://ericps.ed.uiuc.edu/eece/reggio.html

The Project Approach —http://www.ualberta.ca/~schard/projects.htm

Reggio Emilia at NAEYC —http://www.nauticom.net/www/cokids/reggio.html

University of Maine —http://www.umaine.edu

### Community contacts

Consult local child care and early childhood educators' networks.

# Working with Families 6

*Gale Fischer and Bridget Murray*

**with Darla Cohen and
Darcee Hume-Thoren as mentors**

When educators discuss the levels of interaction between parents and teachers, they often use the term *parent involvement*. This term may conjure up images of parents attending teacher-parent meetings and helping at bake sales. However, in most early childhood programs, the parent role—and the relationship between parents and teacher—is far more powerful than that.

Families are the wellspring that creates and nurtures the children in our classrooms. Through many changing classrooms and teachers, parents are the constant in their children's lives. When educators work closely with families, fostering their sense of belonging and their confidence, we strengthen parents' capacity to support their children over a lifetime.

Teachers work toward the development of mutually supportive relationships with the families of the children in their programs. These relationships empower both the families and the teachers, acknowledging the knowledge and strengths of each and emphasizing their common goals. Building such relationships isn't always easy. Families may have very different expectations and styles from those of the teacher. Parents may also bring negative attitudes and feelings about school and teachers based on their own childhood experiences. Communicating effectively and working together successfully may require a lot of effort, but the rewards can be great. We gain increased understanding of the children we teach, and we contribute to a lasting legacy of family support for each child.

And we often learn more about ourselves in the bargain, as the teachers in the following pages describe.

**Gale Fischer** believes that working with parents has been his biggest learning experience and thinks that this might be true for many teachers. **Bridget Murray,** a preschool owner, continues to expand her role as educator and advocate for young children by working for their families and improving their communities.

*—Darla Cohen and Darcee Hume-Thoren*

# Gale Fischer

Gale Fischer

Some key experiences over my years of teaching have changed my view of the relationship between families and teachers. Though I had been taught about the importance of good teacher-parent relationships, I did not really believe at first that this was particularly vital to the child's successful school year. In truth, I saw the teacher as the all-knowing one responsible for the proper education of the child. The parents, if active participants, were there to support the efforts of teachers and then only at the teacher's specific request.

This view may sound a bit extreme, but I truly felt the teacher was the more important partner in the relationship. Now I realize the family is the child's first and main teacher. We are partners that share the same goal: the development and well-being of the child. This realization came through a variety of experiences.

Looking back on events, my first contact with parents occurred in parent-teacher conferences during my stint as a student teacher. After all the conferences were finished, I couldn't stop musing over the fact that in most cases the mother, not the father, attended the conference. I remember thinking to myself, "Don't these fathers care about what is going on in their child's education?"

I realize now how simplistically I viewed the family and its responsibilities and stresses. I did not understand the complexity of family life nor the uniqueness of each family. I was very quick to make judgments about just how families should participate. Through my student-teaching experiences, however, I did learn that teachers don't always make it easy for parents to become involved in their child's education. At times it almost seemed schools and teachers tried to keep parents at arm's length. For example, although the school considered parent-teacher conferences very important for all parents to attend and gave each family several appointment times from which to choose, there was one catch — all appointments were during the school day.

I now believe schools need to put much more effort into being family friendly. We need to consider families' work schedules, child

*Gale Fischer*, M.A., has been a home-based early intervention teacher and a teacher for preschool children with special needs. Currently he teaches preschool children with developmental delays in a public school in Battle Creek, Michigan, as well as teaching gymnastics to preschoolers.

care or sitter requirements, transportation, and so forth if we really want to encourage a strong family-teacher relationship.

Another experience affected my views on parent-teacher relationships. I spent one summer as a lead teacher in a school-age child care setting. Going into this situation, I thought it would be very easy to communicate regularly with family members because they would be there on a daily basis. I was wrong. Arriving tired and rushed, few parents approached me to ask about their child's day. If they had concerns, they usually bypassed me and discussed these with the program director. I often thought, "It would be helpful if they would take the time to talk to me." In retrospect, I think I did not engage parents in discussion because I just didn't know how to begin a conversation and used the busy end-of-the-day activities as an excuse.

One child in my group, an adopted boy with a history of abuse, was taking medication for hyperactivity. Each afternoon I struggled with what I could say about this child's day without being negative, but my responses to the father's questions usually seemed to reveal the child's "bad" behavior. Perhaps I was even setting the stage for conflict between them later, I worried. Although I wanted to change this, I wasn't sure how. I grappled with this dilemma but never resolved it. On the one hand, I believed it was important for parents to have a true picture of their child's day. But, on the other hand, it seemed that reporting so many negative behaviors put added stress on the parent, the child, and the relationship.

## Reaching out to parents for help

After my experiences in child care, I stepped into the world of substitute teaching. I taught in many school districts and at several grade levels. Shortly after Christmas I began substituting in a third-grade class for a teacher on extended leave. The situation was difficult from the beginning. Very few of the children accepted me as their teacher. Having been told that their teacher would be back sometime during the year, the children seemed to feel that we were marking time until the regular teacher's return.

The harder I worked, the less I felt in control. Since it was my first teaching job, I was reluctant to admit I was having any difficulties. I wanted to be able to manage my classroom on my own with no help from other teachers or the principal. I certainly didn't consider parents as a potential source of help. As I struggled I felt I couldn't talk to anyone, not even my wife. I was going to go it alone.

In the class was a girl, Susan, who exhibited the most atypical behaviors I had ever encountered up to that point. She craved attention from adults and peers but really didn't know how to get it. The

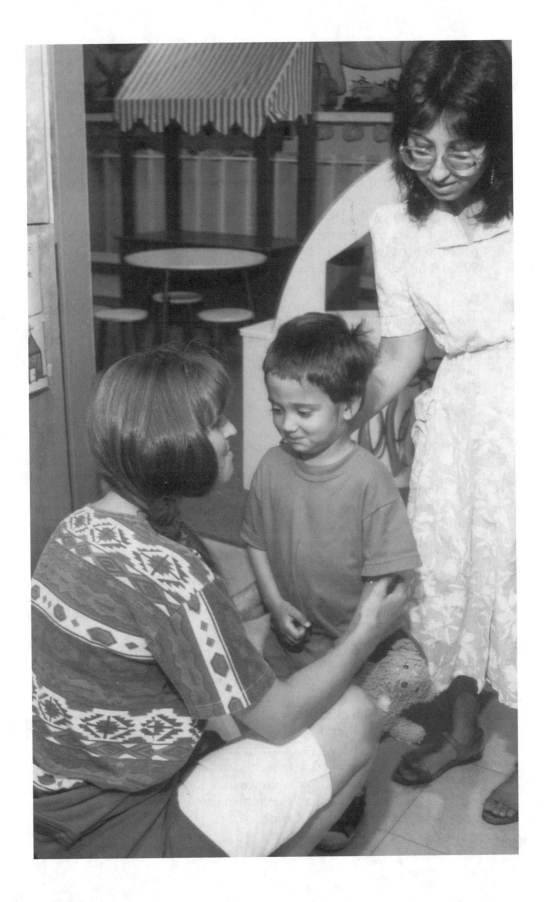

other children often picked on Susan, and she often joined in. When they ignored her, she would make fun of herself to gain attention. Then when the jibes got to be too much, she would cry or vent her anger by yelling, "I hate you! I hate all of you!" Of course, I tried to discourage the teasing and tormenting as well as Susan's attention-getting behaviors, but these patterns had been established long before I came to the classroom.

One source of help I had overlooked was Susan's parents. I was determined to solve this problem on my own — until Susan started venting her anger by throwing her eyeglasses across the room. When this first occurred, I called Susan's mother to explain what had happened to her glasses, and she said she would discuss the matter with Susan. I hoped that would be enough to stop the behavior. It was not. The next step was to have a conference with Susan's parents. Her mother told me that when Susan was younger she was molested by two members of her family. With the school social worker's help, I gathered information for the parents regarding counseling for Susan. Soon she started counseling sessions, and I kept in close contact with her parents through phone calls and conferences. The relationship we developed was positive and beneficial to us all. I was learning to reach out and encouraging the family to reach out as well.

## Gaining interpersonal skills and confidence

In my next teaching position, I had a half-day class of kindergartners, most of whom lived in the neighborhood and walked to and from school with their parents. In many cases, this was the child's first school experience, so parents and children were excited and communicative. Also, a succession of teachers had previously been assigned to this class; I was going to provide a bit of permanence. The parents, thankful for my being there, made me feel comfortable, and I frequently had pleasant, informal chats with them. These casual interactions made it easier, I found, to talk about more vital issues when the time came that this was needed.

After more district reshuffling, I took a preschool special education position. I began the year as a resource/community teacher —many of our preschool children were placed in community preschools — spending one hour a week with each child. Other resource teachers told me that for each child, they alternated between classroom visits and home visits. At first, I was nervous at the prospect of home visits, but I found parents easy to work with and developed a good rapport with them. When I worked with a child at school, I always sent a note home to let the parents know what we had done that day. Even as my case load increased, I kept up the home visits because I was convinced they were worth the time and effort.

## Learning from families

*One source of help I had overlooked was Susan's parents. I was determined to solve this problem on my own.*

To keep my job, I was required to take course work in early childhood or special education. In the early childhood special education program at Indiana University, I began a course stressing a family-focused approach to teaching. Everything we discussed in class seemed to relate directly to something on the job that day and provided valuable insights. In my classroom I had been assigned a new student named Jay. Reading through Jay's file, I learned that his parents, too, had been in special education programs throughout their school years. I decided to make a home visit, wondering whether Jay's parents would be what I considered to be good parents.

On most of my visits, Jay's grandparents and sometimes even an aunt or uncle were there in addition to his parents. When I arrived the family immediately turned off the television, and everyone tuned in to what Jay and I were doing. I felt they were eager to learn what they could from me. Quickly I discovered that I was learning from them as well. Family members made helpful comments like, "This week Jay worked on this" or "Jay does better when it is done this way." I began asking them questions about Jay. And I was learning that a family's caring about education and, even more important, their care and concern for the child were invaluable to the child and to me as the teacher.

During one afternoon home visit with Jay and his family, his father received an urgent phone call and had to leave abruptly. He was very apologetic about needing to leave, though I tried to reassure him. After he left, Jay's grandmother said she wanted me to know that her son was trying to do the best he could as a parent. After that day, the grandmother and I spoke often about many different issues. We were of two different backgrounds, two different generations, but we both cared about Jay.

The next year I was a classroom teacher in the morning and a resource teacher in the afternoon. One day, while I worked with Don, who used a respirator and oxygen machine 24 hours a day, the lights in his home flickered and then went off. Immediately warning lights and sirens started on the respirator and oxygen machine. Instantly, Don's mother was in the room working with his machines. Only the oxygen machine had a back-up battery system, which she hooked up immediately. A quick phone call to the power company revealed that the power was out throughout the neighborhood. Don's mother explained the urgent situation but was told that power could not be restored for at least an hour. She unhooked him from the machine and began to use a bag-type device to squeeze oxygen into his system. She continued for five minutes, then decided to try the machine again.

She and the nurse thought he was turning pale, and he kept trying to unhook the machine and grab the bag. I felt panicky, but Don's mother didn't; she had a definite plan to respond to each reaction from him. Two hours after the electricity went off, she called the ambulance, calmly and clearly explaining the conditions and answering the paramedics' questions. This experience opened my eyes to the challenges and stresses Don's parents —and, in different ways, all parents —live with.

## Striving for positive change

The summer before becoming a classroom and resource teacher, I gave considerable thought to how I could build good relationships with the families of my classroom children as well as the families of children in community preschools, for whom I served as resource teacher. I considered making monthly visits to each child's home but realized that, as a classroom teacher, my schedule would make this very difficult. I started by making a home visit to each child before

school started. By spring I had made three or four home visits to each of the classroom children. Developing close relationships with my classroom families was more challenging than it was with my community families, but I worked at it.

The family of a child named Eric, who had cerebral palsy, taught me a lot about overcoming barriers that seem insurmountable. Eric had typically developing mental capabilities but limited physical capabilities. He could crawl but not walk and used a wheelchair but not independently.

Four or five weeks after Eric joined the class, we received free passes to the zoo. But it happened with very short notice, and transportation for the children with special needs, all of whom were in the morning program, could not be arranged, so they were unable to participate. I accepted the situation. When I was talking with Eric's mom a few days later, she questioned our leaving out the children with special needs. Although she voiced her questions and opinions calmly, she made me realize that what had happened was a form of discrimination, and I had been a party to it.

Later in the year another scheduled field trip presented the problem of transportation for the morning classes. I discussed our options with the preschool director, suggesting that a note be sent home about the field trip and explaining that children could participate if parents picked them up at school after the trip. We wouldn't have enough staff for the trip if several of the children with special needs came, so we asked for volunteers. We took the time to work toward a satisfactory solution for all, and Eric's mother was very pleased with our efforts. Her confronting me about inclusion led to my exploring possible solutions that worked for everyone. Experiences like this one have changed my attitudes and opinions, my actions and interactions.

# Gale's mentor reflects . . .

Like many teachers, Gale entered the profession without parenting experience and began to build an understanding of families. Initially he found it difficult to ask for help from anyone.

The role of parents that Gale first perceived was one of being responsive when and if he made requests of them. He tells us how quick he was to make assumptions and form judgments about the values, priorities, or abilities of family members. Through some of the experiences he recounts, Gale began to look differently at families, not jump to conclusions, and keep an open mind.

Home visits, he says, did a lot to transform his initial view of parent participation. He began to recognize the family as the child's first and main teacher and appreciate the needs and often invisible emotional issues many families face.

Teachers don't always make it easy for parents to become involved in their children's education, Gale admits. He discusses what he sees as the catch-22 of involving families in school: If school functions occur after school, the teachers and staff work overtime and are away from their own families. On the other hand, if school functions occur during school hours, parents working outside the home may never be able to participate and as a result feel less involved. Having honest, ongoing discussions with families about what works can help resolve such dilemmas.

Gale has talked with us about learning how to support families in the many challenges they encounter, from simple lack of time to more complex personal demands and issues. Many of these challenges cannot be handled by quick fixes, but teachers help when they strive to be aware, empathetic, and supportive.

Knowing when to ask for help is a strength, not a weakness, which Gale has learned. Teachers should allow themselves to ask questions, debate possibilities, discuss alternatives with colleagues, and plan and develop strategies with parents. Meeting the needs of families requires seeing each family as it truly is, not as it may appear from first impression.

**T**hink about your childhood experiences in school. Were your parents involved as partners with the school? How did the school convey expectations about parents' roles in their children's schooling?

**D**raw a square on a large sheet of paper. Write inside it a list of the efforts you make (or those made by a program with which you are familiar) to build partnerships with families. Next, brainstorm other possible methods of family support, participation, and communication, and add the ideas in the margins outside the square.

**D**raw or create with a medium such as pipe cleaners a symbol or other type of representation of families. Share your representations with others. How are your representations similar or different?

**T**ake three sheets of paper and on the first, write your goals for children. On the second, write what you believe are parents' goals. Use the third sheet to create a common-ground goals list. Think about the three lists and how they relate to your work with parents.

W hen first I started my preschool program, I had little formal knowledge of early childhood education. My cues came from the parents of the children enrolled. These parents wanted so much for their children. They were eager for their children to do well in school. So I believed it was my job to teach, and the parents were the major influence on my curriculum.

The feelings of insecurity I developed in this situation prompted me to seek further training in early childhood education. In searching for provider education, I read that CDA (Child Development Associate) classes were being offered at a nearby university. I enrolled and began learning how to operate a child care program as a professional. These classes gave me my first formal training in working with families.

Before opening my program, I had developed enrollment forms to gain basic, necessary information about the children entering my program. Through my CDA training, I discovered how much more I needed to know. I revised the forms to provide more insight into each child's personality, likes and dislikes, and special interests. I wanted the new forms to serve as tools to enable me to know the children in my program better and work with their families more effectively, and it did help. Yet, I knew it was not nearly enough. To support every child's development, I knew that I needed to build a strong relationship with the family of each child in my program.

## Establishing relationships

I started by making a conscious effort to connect personally with each parent, grandparent, or family member as he or she came to the program. I would say, "Courtney is really looking forward to your trip to California. She tells me you are leaving next week." I conveyed concern by commenting, "Johnny has been draggy today. You might want to keep an eye on him to see if he's getting sick or needs more sleep." The more interaction I initiated, the more the parents appeared comfortable in sharing their knowledge and concerns. They were becoming a valuable resource.

*Bridget Murray, B.S., has owned her own preschool for 20 years and teaches Child Development Associate (CDA) classes in southern Indiana.*

In my interactions I always tried to convey three ideas: the value of the child, the family's important role in the child's life, and my commitment to both the child and the family. At first I had to think of ways I could convey these messages. Now words come more naturally. Continuing to build beyond these simple exchanges to develop meaningful working relationships with the children's families is my goal. Strong relationships with parents are especially important when a child has special needs.

Spending many hours a day with the children, I observe behaviors and patterns that may be useful for parents for know about. Having ongoing lines of communication enables us to talk when either a parent or I have questions or concerns and not only when a real problem has developed.

At one point I was caring for a child who seemed to be showing developmental delay in some areas. Because I had built a strong relationship with the mother, I felt comfortable sharing my observations and concerns. The mother told me the child had experienced complications at birth, and I encouraged her to seek professional assessment and guidance. Although she agreed, her husband did not, and their difference of opinion created tension between them. This was their situation to resolve; my role was to inform and support.

I have come to view myself as a resource for the families with whom I work. Seeing families in need of assistance, I try to refer them to appropriate agencies or individuals who can help. Knowing the families well helps me to know how and when to offer support. There are times when families want help but are hesitant to ask. There are also those times when families may identify their needs differently than I do and not want assistance.

## Building bridges in busy times

Building relationships with busy working parents has been a challenge at times. All of them are balancing and juggling many demands. Quite a few of the children in my program are brought and picked up by someone other than a parent: a caregiver, another family member, or a friend of the family. Some parents in our rural county work many miles away and must leave home before my preschool opens and return after it has closed. I have learned the importance of making special efforts for these parents —writing personal notes, providing newsletters, and letting them know I'm happy to talk with them at their convenience. I use a large bulletin board to post announcements, yard-sale notices, want ads, carpool requests, and so on.

My role as a resource to parents has included calling their attention to workshops that provide useful information and even referring them to local organizations that offer assistance for workshop registration and travel fees. I try to keep parents up-to-date on parent-focused television and radio programs and magazine articles about aspects of family life. I make available brochures and books on topics from nutrition to balancing home and work responsibilities, sharing, and carpooling.

## Sharing information about children's learning

Another part of working with parents is communicating my philosophy of teaching and sharing information regarding appropriate practice in early childhood programs. Parents want what is best for their children. They want them to be successful but often believe that very didactic methods pave the road to that success. At the beginning of the year, I introduce my philosophy of early childhood education so that parents can better understand why we do what we do in our preschool.

I understand parents' strong desire to emphasize what were once called the "basics" through worksheets and drill. Many of us received our education this way: teacher in the front teaching, children quiet and working, pencils in hand. Now I understand that young children learn best through active engagement with materials and other people, but many parents have different ideas. It is part of my job to communicate to parents what and how their children are learning through our classroom activities and environment.

At every opportunity I emphasize the importance of the parents, the child's first teachers. I try to build a bridge between what we do at preschool and what parents can do at home with their child. "I don't know how to teach my child. I'm not a teacher," I often hear. I am constantly working to convey to parents that a child can learn through natural interaction, that learning does not require sitting with pencil in hand. When sharing materials with the families, I often introduce the game, book, or activity to the child just before he goes home. Then the child will teach the game or "read" the story first, and parents will take a turn next.

To encourage active involvement, I begin by asking parents to fill out a parent resource form or talking with them informally about their interests. While encouraging involvement, I try to avoid adding to the endless demands put on families today. Some parents feel frustrated that they can't participate in field trips or classroom activity because of their work schedules. One method we have developed is for such parents to tape stories at home in the evening for children to listen to during the day at the listening center. Children love telling their friends that their mom, dad, grandma, or grandpa is reading at the listening center.

## Reaping the benefits

Getting family members involved helps me as well. Having parents or grandparents in the classroom as volunteers enhances children's learning opportunities. They provide an often-needed extra pair of hands; they can interact and support children's play, serve as resources, and give me the insights and information about their own children that enable me to do better individualizing of experiences.

Seeing their families involved with their classroom, children feel their learning experiences are valued. Parents become more aware of

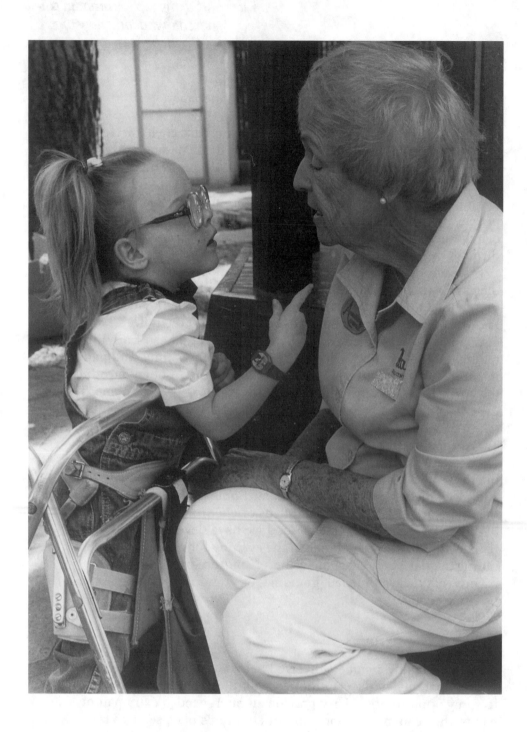

what to expect and encourage in terms of appropriate practice in their child's education. They feel a part of the child's new world and can see their child in a variety of new ways.

## The journey continues

All of these benefits derive from true and honest relationships, developed over time. To me it is important not to settle for superficial parent involvement. Communication and interaction with families must be nurtured, and though these are not always easy or comfortable, they are always worthwhile.

With increased training opportunities in my state, I have more chances to enhance my skills and knowledge base regarding family relations and support. Over time, I have become a strong advocate for the children and families I serve. I know I need to keep up-to-date and well informed on family and children's issues. Participating in formal training experiences, informal collaborations with other colleagues, and personal reading have aided my learning. When issues affecting children and families are debated or discussed, I feel empowered to stand for their rights and lobby for change to improve their quality of life. One way in which I serve is as the coordinator of an organization working to meet the needs of children and families in our county. This involvement allows me the opportunity to promote positive change, increase public awareness of children's issues, and collaborate with others interested in the welfare of young children. Although there is still much to know, I feel more confident in expressing my opinions and voicing my concerns because of the learning experiences I have had in recent years.

Children's lives seem to be more complex as time goes on. Many are hurried into academic and extracurricular activities in   which they are expected to excel; others are exposed early to adult lifestyles and situations. From a young age, children may have to deal with family problems and behave as adults. I worry that many children are not receiving the nurturing they need to grow and mature into healthy and happy adults, largely as a result of the pressures of modern life on families. This is why, in promoting the development of children in my program, I focus on supporting and encouraging the positive efforts of families.

# Bridget's mentor reflects ...

Bridget writes about friendly and respectful informal communication as the first layer of a relationship. With this foundation she then works to build the strong relationship that allows her and the parent to have more substantive dialogues and negotiate from different perspectives to solve problems.

Bridget often discussed in her mentor conversations that as educators we have to try to see a family as the family members see themselves. She was recognizing too the importance of working with families to identify shared goals for the child rather than just assuming we know what's best for the child. "Are these the goals of the family or my goals?" we must ask ourselves. If I have goals for the child, I need to share them with the family and discuss how I'm working on them when the child is with me. And I need to listen to parents' goals for their children and take them seriously.

Bridget finds that families' goals, although they may express them differently, often are the same as those we have as teachers. If parents ask for worksheets to use at home to help ensure their child's learning, for example, the teacher can turn this into an opportunity to increase their understanding of developmentally appropriate methods of achieving learning goals. She can share information about how children learn and the many ways parents can encourage learning in the home without using worksheets. The goal of teacher and parent is the same—both want the child to learn.

**W**rite about a teacher, director, or other professional who has created a positive atmosphere of welcome for parents. Describe what that individual or program does that helps create these relationships. If you are a teacher, which of these strategies do you use in your program?

**F**rom your own teaching experience, recount a success story that involved some interaction with a child's family. Think about the family involved and factors that went into ensuring this successful relationship. Consider what you learned from this experience and how you might apply this information in relation to other families. Assess the problems you encountered along the way and how you solved them.

**W**hat metaphor or analogy do you see as characterizing families? Can you suggest another metaphor to describe working with families? In a group or as part of a team, discuss these metaphors with your colleagues. What do they tell you about the role you expect of and share with families?

**W**ith others, discuss ways to enhance your work with families. What are the problems or roadblocks? How can you address these problems in your relationships with parents?

## *Resources for further exploration of this topic*

### Books and periodicals

Clifford, R.M. 1997. Partnerships with families. *Young Children* 52 (3): 2.

Diffily, D., & K. Morrison, eds. 1996. *Family-friendly communication for early childhood programs.* Washington, DC: NAEYC.

*Exceptional Parent.* A monthly magazine for families and professionals (P.O. Box 3000, Dept. EP, Denville, NJ 07834; 800-562-1973).

Felber, S.A. 1997. Strategies for parent partnerships. *Teaching Exceptional Children* (Sept./Oct.): 20–23.

Powell, D.R. 1989. *Families and early childhood programs.* Washington, DC: NAEYC.

Roberts, R.N., S. Rule, & M.S. Innocenti. 1998. *Strengthening the family-professional partnership in services for young children.* Baltimore, MD: Paul H. Brookes.

Seligman, M., & R.B. Darling. 1997. *Ordinary families, special children.* 2d ed. New York: Guilford.

Springate, K.W., & D.A. Stegelin. In press. *Building school and community partnerships through parent involvement.* Upper Saddle River, NJ: Merrill.

### Videotapes

*Partnerships with parents.* 1989. 28 min. Washington, DC: NAEYC.

*They don't come with manuals.* 1987. 29 min. New York: Insight Media (212-721-6316).

*Young children: Our hope for the future.* 1989. 55 min. Speech by James P. Comer. Washington, DC: NAEYC.

### Websites

*Exceptional Parent*—http://www.pedianet.com/news/resource/eparent/index.html

The National Information Center for Children and Youth with Disabilities (NICHCY)—http://www.nichcy.org

National Parent Information Network—http://www.npin.org

### Community contacts

Consult your state department of education and/or university or college department of special education to identify local- and state-level parent advocacy organizations or networks.

# Collaboration 7

*Mary Horn, Sheila Pluckebaum,
and Blanca Bandera and Patty Burke*

*with Tamyra Freeman as mentor*

The widely quoted adage "It takes a whole village to
raise a child" may sound like an overstatement, but it's
true. Some problems we face as early childhood educators really are too big and too complex for us to solve
individually. Studies of creative problem solving and
group process confirm that effective groups can accomplish more than any one of the talented individuals who
compose them. In providing the best service to children,
we are better off when we "hold hands and stick together."

Collaborative skills are coming to be recognized as
critical tools for early childhood educators and special
educators. Increasingly, educators are being asked to
work in new ways with other professionals and with the
families of children in their care. Doing so doesn't
always come easily, as the writers in this chapter found
out. Our assumption that other team members think as we
do and know the same things runs into reality: they often
do not. Immediately we are challenged to rethink many of
our attitudes and beliefs. In the process we often gain new
perspectives, develop new skills, and generate new solutions to tough problems.

**Mary Horn** became especially interested in the topic
of collaboration when she took a new job as the administrator of an early intervention program. She quickly
realized that her goals for developing services that
would work well for children and families could be
achieved only through collaboration. **Sheila Pluckebaum**
saw the need to strengthen her collaborative skills when

she was asked to assume new roles as her school system began implementing programs to enable preschool children with disabilities to learn alongside typically developing peers. **Blanca Bandera** and **Patty Burke** call their experience with collaboration "overwhelmingly positive." For more than three years, they worked together in supporting several young children with special needs to participate successfully in a community preschool. As a duo they share what has been important to them in building a strong collaborative relationship.

*—Tamyra Freeman*

# Mary Horn

Mary Horn

I t wasn't until I became director of children's services that I first
stumbled upon the many challenges of collaboration. I started in
the position with many opinions about the way things should be
for children with special needs, their families, and the agency's staff.
Immediately I was bombarded with issues that were at odds with my
vision. If our program was going to provide quality services, I quickly
realized I needed to build strong relationships with and between the
staff and the families we served. I learned as I went along.

I believed I was entering my new director position as a well-
rounded individual who could draw from past experiences when
making decisions. I had risen through the ranks at the same work-
place, a developmental disability agency. As a high-schooler, I started
as an assistant and later held positions as substitute teacher, infant
teacher, and preschool teacher of children with special needs. I had
qualifications, but was I prepared for leadership?

In my years as a teacher, I often had worked with doctors, therapists, psychologists, social workers, other teachers, parent advocates,
and special education cooperatives, but I never thought that what we
were doing was collaboration. I didn't encounter the concept of
collaboration explicitly until I became involved with our state's First
Steps program, which provides early intervention services to infants and toddlers. I remember a speaker for that program stating
that successful collaborations must build on relationships of
respect and trust. I liked her emphasis on "building" (which acknowledged that collaboration is an ongoing process), and she
helped me see that collaboration requires equal ownership and
input from all parties involved.

Unfortunately I didn't apply these helpful tips when I started in
my new position. In taking the position I knew I had my work cut out
for me. Our agency provides services to five rural counties. Our two
sites are located a 45-minute travel distance apart and operate in two
different time zones. Not only do distance and time create barriers,
but each site is quite unique.

*Mary Horn*, B.A., was an early intervention teacher and is now the director
of children's services at Comprehensive Developmental Centers that serves
five rural counties in northwestern Indiana.

In all my previous experience with the agency, I had worked at only one site. I had heard stories about the conflict that went on at the other site, and saw this for myself on my first visit there as director. Whenever I made suggestions, I got the same response from nearly every staff person, "This is the way we've always done it." Hearing this attitude voiced again and again, I knew that it was going to be hard to shake. I felt compelled to focus on this lack of vision and facilitate intrasite collaboration.

I decided to approach the differing attitudes between the sites by holding a joint meeting and delivering a pep talk. In this talk I shared information about my educational background and history with the agency. I also expressed empathy in regard to our "overworked and underpaid" reality and tried to update staff on legislative proposals that might affect our operation. I acknowledged the challenges of effective communication between the two sites but let them know my door and phone line would always be open. I likened myself to a basketball coach —the staff was my team, with some being good dribblers, others better foul shooters, but all of us a team. The floor was open for discussion, and no one had issues to address.

## Making mistakes and learning from them

Word got back to me that some staff felt I had spoken too much and hadn't really listened. I realized I had spoken rapidly in my nervousness, but I thought the comments about not listening were unfair. Hadn't I asked for questions? They didn't speak up, and the smiles on their faces had led me to believe they understood and concurred with what I was saying. Yet I could see that I was respon-sible for most of what happened. I had looked at things from my own viewpoint and had set the meeting's agenda with little opportunity for staff input.

I realized I had to have another meeting soon and do things very differently. This time I sent a memo asking staff to participate in setting the date and creating the agenda. I started the meeting more informally by allowing everybody to say a little bit about themselves as individuals and the roles each filled in her own family and commu-nity. The sharing helped us feel closer. Staff from the two sites then generated a list of concerns that I recorded on flip charts and re-sponded to as best I could. I was encouraged to think we were on our way as a team. I repeated my invitation for staff members to phone or stop by. They accepted my invitation —and *how!*

I began to get phone calls left and right, and at first I was pleased. But I was hearing "tattling" (in the name of betterment of the program), and I was often put in the position of choosing sides. I suggested holding weekly meetings to discuss how the staff were working together. They needed to address issues related to their own classrooms and interactions with one another —brainstorm instead of "blamestorm." Written summaries from their meetings would help me identify issues that were pervasive across the agency. All were given the latitude to ask me directly to facilitate a meeting if they had tried giving one another objective feedback and reached a dead end.

*If staff are to work together effectively, we must have opportunities to reflect on how our educational, experiential, and philosophical differences affect our work.*

This system has worked well for the most part, though I am still concerned that some staff are too reticent. For the time being I am addressing only those issues brought to me through defined communication channels (in hopes of nurturing a collaborative spirit) instead of acting on hearsay.

## Common ground

Many meetings later the communication between myself and the program staff continues to be filled with learning for us all. I am planning intensive training initiatives to address the issues identified in our meetings. I am beginning to see that if staff are to work together effectively, we must have opportunities to reflect on how our educational, experiential, and philosophical differences affect our work. I am seeing the benefits of empowerment and respect.

Focusing on what our agency's mission statement says about respecting and trusting each other and the families we work with, I have tried to encourage the staff to believe in their capability to give and receive objective feedback. I discuss issues related to the future of the children's program with the staff and try not to dictate my own version. Each staff member's opinion and background help shape the experiences families have in our program.

It has been a struggle to get people with many years of experience to be open to suggestions from those less experienced. The hierarchies built into many of our service models have become more evident to me and are a challenge. In addition to our classroom-based services, we also have a home-teacher program that enables families to learn new ways to support their infant's or toddler's development at home. For years staff members have disagreed as to which approach is better for families, and I became concerned when this conflict reached families themselves. Classroom teachers often were accused of not respecting families and the issues and stresses families have to deal with in their lives. Home teachers came under attack for being so personally close with families that they failed to address critical health

and safety issues in the home (for fear the families would stop participating in the program).

A recent experience helped me understand better the different roles of the home teacher and classroom teacher. At school a young child went into a seizure. The ambulance came, the mother arrived and rode with the classroom teacher, and I followed. Later when our home teacher arrived, it was obvious the mother was relieved to see her. They talked and the mom filled her in on everything that was happening. We waited and waited with the family.

As I drove home after four grueling hours at the hospital, I felt the force of this experience. I was aware of the powerful experiences home teachers share with families and the bond they form. Events such as this put these teachers in touch with a family's life in a way rarely experienced by classroom teachers, who typically see families only in a professional environment. We are trying to develop across our programs a shared philosophy about what it means to truly support families and to respect all the various ways of providing support, each valuable in its own way.

## Trust and respect

Recently a new staff member remarked that she had trouble respecting families who "didn't care." "Why do you say they don't care?" I asked. She described a child often sent to school unkempt and with a poor lunch. I told her how I can't personally do everything for my children if a school morning is too hectic. Acknowledging that sometimes I too am upset about some of the children's living conditions, I said that I feel we need to be careful not to make assumptions that those conditions are wrong.

I encourage my staff to look at how their own backgrounds and beliefs affect how they react to and support families. We often react to issues based on our own beliefs when dealing with the world, and *if* we don't broaden our experiences, we jeopardize our ability to be effective with families.

I began to see that some staff struggles result from different philosophies and assumptions. One teacher's action might be viewed negatively by another simply because the latter didn't realize or share the philosophy underlying the action. For example, one classroom teacher devoted a lot of time to phoning parents to discuss what they could do to help their child. The home teacher saw no point in this because she believed it was essential to help the family first before intervening with the child.

In turn, I am learning to use the strengths of different perspectives instead of just trying to get people to see things from one view or my own view as director. For example, we have needs in our rural area for parent support and training groups. To facilitate the start-up of parent groups, we need the participation of the staff members whose strengths are in these areas. I have shared my visions with them and asked that they share theirs with me.

## New ways to communicate

My hopes are high that our lines of communication are opening up. I am committed to creating more opportunities for experienced staff and new teachers to talk together about how best to support families and improve services to children. As this happens, we reduce hierarchies based on experience level. We are all trying to learn to present our opinions in constructive ways. If as a staff we work toward defining our shared set of priorities and guidelines, we then will be better able to involve parents in the process.

One thing I've come to see is that this is not a cut-and-dried world. In becoming a reflective practitioner, I am always trying to see how my own behaviors and attitudes should change. I am working to encourage this same habit of reflection in those around me. I believe the collaborative process is a worthy one —it just doesn't come with directions.

# Mary's mentor reflects . . .

Mary found that her move from teaching to an administrative position required her to examine some of her basic assumptions about how people work together to achieve a common goal. During our conversations about collaboration, Mary and I struggled to better understand how professionals can partner with families to best support each child's development.

One of the first issues we explored was how prominently values and culture affect every person's beliefs about education and child development. To collaborate effectively we must learn to respect the beliefs of our co-workers, professionals from different backgrounds, and the families in our programs. We need to explore how our own viewpoints and preferences have been shaped by our families, neighbors, co-workers, religious organizations, and other personally important factors. Mary and I talked about how our own culture, ethnicity, socioeconomic level, language, and educational experiences influence each of us and our biases. As Mary discovered when she began encouraging and supporting staff in exploring their own beliefs, the simple act of recognizing the differences in our viewpoints is a key step in enhancing a team's ability to work together.

Finding common ground to build upon is important not only in our interactions with each other as professionals but also in our relationships with families. In my own roles I am continually struggling to understand what structures and processes can be put in place so that professionals in education/child development, health care, and social services work together with families as equal partners. I have come to believe that when the family is seen as the child's foremost teacher, a natural collaboration will often occur between family members and service providers. When we work alongside parents with genuine respect for their contributions, priorities, and concerns, we help to build the trust and respect that is necessary for a true partnership.

Think about the adults in your own life. How did they work collaboratively? What were the elements that helped or hurt this collaboration? Relate this to your own collaborative efforts.

After you have spent some time thinking about your own style, think about a colleague you work with. Do your styles match, conflict, or complement each other? Take some time to discuss your styles and talk about the best ways for you to communicate.

Make a web focusing on the child as the center. Add all the people who touch the child's life. Think about the connection—or lack of connection—between all the other people in this child's life. Think about how your role fits in this web.

If you are now participating on a team with other professionals and with parents, individually create a symbol or representation to represent your philosophy on serving children and their families. Meet with team members and share your symbols. How are they similar and different. What have you learned about your shared goals and what about your differences?

L ooking back over the past school years, I realize that it has been a period of transition for me like no other I have experienced —exceptionally filled with challenges, struggles, growth, and reflection.

My professional role has had many facets, from teaching in an urban public school system for preschool children with special needs, to implementing a program supporting typically developing preschoolers from the neighborhood in joining our classroom. During this same period, I co-taught a large classroom of preschoolers with special needs and served as resource teacher for 3- to 5-year-olds with special needs who were attending community preschools. Each role required me to collaborate with others to be effective, and I have found it is not an easy or automatic process.

I've always thought I had a gift for enjoying, appreciating, and getting along well with others. When I first realized I would be involved in various collaborative efforts, I was excited about the possibilities but also a little anxious.

At the start of the second year, a dear friend and fellow preschool teacher, Sharon, and I designed a peer-model program to involve typically developing preschoolers in our classroom. Neighborhood children would be good role models in play and communication, we thought, for the preschoolers with special needs.

Having researched many similar initiatives, we knew that a key component of effective programs is consistent involvement of parents in the classroom. Since the two of us had both been involved in cooperative preschools, we felt comfortable and confident in encouraging more parental involvement in our respective classrooms. With each of the enrolling families, we spoke about parental involvement, and parents were enthusiastic.

Then school began. When we asked parents to actually commit to a time to be in the classroom, they often responded that they couldn't that week but would definitely do it the next week. When the next week came, the same thing happened. With the extra children from neighborhood programs in the class, we had more children but too few adults.

*Sheila Pluckebaum, M.S., has been involved in early intervention, supporting infants, toddlers, and preschoolers with special needs in home-based, community-based, and classroom programs in the greater Indianapolis area for six years.*

*We spoke about parent involvement. When we asked parents to commit to a time to be in the classroom, they often responded that they couldn't that week.*

We realized we had not explained thoroughly how important parents' participation was to the program. In trying to develop collaboration with parents, we had failed to establish a shared understanding of what all of us were working toward. Likewise, we had not set up open and comfortable lines of communication. Sharon and I were focused on the children; we assumed the adults' roles would fall into place. What we learned is to assume nothing, take nothing for granted.

After better communication was established, we learned that another program needed a room. Since my enrollment was low, the logical choice was for me to teach with Sharon in her classroom.

The previous year Sharon and I often brought our classes together for long periods of time, and that had worked well. With children who needed more individualized support and personal space, however, we were apprehensive about a combined class full time. But we had no choice in this matter, whether or not we thought it was best for the children, and, given our friendship, shared philosophies, and senses of humor, we thought we could manage.

Looking back, I can see that problems were bound to arise in a collaboration entered into so blindly and passively.

## Experiencing differences with a colleague

Sharon and I shared a commitment to providing a positive, nurturing environment for young children of all developmental levels. We believed in using patience, gentleness, respect, choices within guidelines, play, and communication to enrich the environment. What we didn't anticipate was how the dynamics of our own teacher-assistant relationships would influence us and how different—and how deeply ingrained—our individual ideas and preferences were. Disappointed in myself that I wasn't handling the change well, I was afraid to talk about my struggles. We had given no thought to how our roles might change and the need to discuss this. We hadn't seen the need to talk in advance about communicating openly when problems or uncomfortable situations arose. Both of us are very accommodating, so we didn't foresee the need to talk about our differences.

Mostly my struggles were over little things, but they started to affect my comfort level. Sharon and I had different viewpoints on some aspects of our collaboration. We worked through issues such as who would do circle time or plan snack, but we didn't discuss keeping activity and noise levels comfortable for everyone. I was struggling with what felt like an issue of control.

Another difficulty coinciding with the activity level was the issue of challenging behaviors. When a particular situation occurred, all four of us (two teachers and two assistants) assumed we would all be responsible. In reality we tended to take primary responsibility for the children we saw as ours though we sometimes talked about the need to get beyond this habit . We struggled to be proactive, but we seemed to be becoming reactive. The situation was challenging and becoming overwhelming to me.

## Making time to talk

By failing to talk through such issues in our collaboration from the outset, we caused problems not only for ourselves but also for our teaching assistants.

About this time our supervisor let us know that I would need to shift to the role of resource teacher supporting preschoolers in community preschools. I had mixed feelings about the change. I was concerned about Sharon and the others with one less pair of hands. I was stressed but decided finally to accept the position as it allowed me to structure my time to pick up my own children from school. I was hopeful that new experiences with parents and teachers in the community settings would be positive and enlightening. Unfortunately I didn't take the time to reflect on my recent experiences and learn from them. I left feeling overwhelmed, a feeling everyone has experienced as a new teacher. My first years of teaching were filled with some times when I felt like an imposter, unqualified to be in charge. As I began to experi-

ence being a support in the community, some of these same feelings surfaced. Most challenging for me has been figuring out how best to support the staff in the community preschools where our preschoolers with special needs are enrolled.

## Collaborating with families

A child named Lilly was placed in a 3-year-olds' program at the YMCA for three afternoons a week, and it was my job to help her make the transition. From my supervisor I learned that the classroom teachers there had worked with children with special needs before, considered Lilly a welcome addition, and felt confident that they could support her needs related to her communication delays.

I began the transition process by making a home visit with Lilly and her family the week before she was to start school. Her mom, dad, grandma, two older siblings, and baby brother were present. The family seemed excited about this opportunity for Lilly. I felt good about my role and comfortable with the support I was giving the family during this initial visit. I explained that I also would visit Lilly's preschool when she had been there a few days.

When I arrived at the preschool, I could tell that the classroom staff were very anxious to see me. Having only seen Lilly in her home setting, I hadn't anticipated her having problems adjusting to the classroom. But apparently she showed many problematic behaviors that never emerged in one-on-one situations.

The teachers and I spoke briefly and decided to continue talking after class. I observed Lilly as the children sat down to eat their snack. She walked around the room, only coming back to the table when she was asked. She would take a bite and then begin walking again. Lilly required physical assistance in making the transition from one activity to another. During group time a classroom assistant directed her to sit on a carpet square. This seemed to give her focus, and the assistant sat behind encouraging her to participate.

After class the teacher gave me her assessment of how Lilly was doing, adding, "I'm not qualified to work with Lilly. I wasn't trained to work with children with needs like hers." I vividly remember her words because I had thought the same many times myself.

I knew that this teacher had the skills it takes. My job was to help her find confidence in handling the situation by supporting her and collaborating with her and the family. At first I tried to encourage the teacher and classroom assistant by reminding them that Lilly was getting used to a new environment and the other children welcoming her. I said the carpet square at circle time was a good strategy. These teachers were dedicated, but exasperated and overwhelmed. The main thing to do, I realized, was to listen.

We decided that another home visit might be helpful in learning what kind of structure Lilly was used to at home. The home visit also would be beneficial to our collaborative efforts with the family. Visiting Lilly's family the next day, I learned a lot. I described Lilly's classroom "wandering" to her mother and grandmother as I explained what her teachers were struggling with at school. Later, playing with Lilly in her room, I saw that nothing kept her attention for longer than a few seconds. She had many toys and had difficulty choosing what to play with.

The family and I talked about the structure they provided in their daily routine. Earlier in the year the family had realized it wasn't a good idea for the children to fall asleep in front of the television, and they initiated a nighttime routine: a game that their older children enjoyed but that Lilly found boring. Snacking at home all day, Lilly didn't come to the table to eat with the family during mealtimes.

Lilly's mother had learning difficulties, I knew, and thus the grandmother was very involved with the children and their well-being. I learned that Lilly's 6-year-old brother had intense emotional difficulties that required occasional hospitalization. I considered how I could best support the family while helping empower them, and I thought about what all of our roles were in this collaboration. What should I expect? I was but the first of many professionals this family would deal with in support of Lilly. My job was to work with both the family and the other professionals toward what was best for Lilly at this time in her development.

Meeting with Lilly's teachers the next day, I shared what I had learned during the home visit. After much deliberation, we concluded that for the moment Lilly might do better in a self-contained classroom with a small number of children who also had disabilities. The school nearest to her home had an excellent program. Lilly could ride the bus every day, taking care of the transportation problems and relieving her mother of worry. A smaller group and lower teacher-to-child ratio would mean less activity, which could be overwhelming to Lilly. She would have experiences that would help her be ready to participate in a community-based classroom.

As I look back on this situation, I realize I had made many assumptions in the beginning. I had relied heavily on the experience of others instead of assessing for myself all the factors involved. For instance, I had not considered the impact of Lilly's mother having learning problems, nor had I anticipated the major barrier that lack of family transportation would be. I had not taken into account the stresses on the family from Lilly's brother's emotional issues and the responsibilities for a young infant at home.

To make this a true collaborative effort, all participants needed to bring their concerns, insights, and information together to provide the basis for deciding how best to support Lilly. In an effective collaboration the insight or information one member of the team does not have is contributed by another.

*If someone had asked me whether I would be an immediately effective participant in a collaborative effort, I would have said yes without hesitation. Nine months later, I realize I was naive.*

## Lifelong learning

If someone had asked me at the beginning of the year whether I thought I would be an immediately effective participant in a collaborative effort, I would have said yes without hesitation. Nine months and several experiences later, I realize I was naive. Through these experiences I've learned and grown personally and professionally. What I have been strongly impressed with is that we are always learning; from each experience we can and should take new understandings and skills into our next encounter.

# Sheila's mentor reflects . . .

Working closely with others often provokes our own reflections and shows us things about ourselves. For a year I closely followed Sheila's career as she took on new roles to support children with disabilities in inclusive settings. I observed how she used new challenges to learn more about herself and her ability to collaborate.

Like Sheila, I often respond to new roles with anxiety—many of us do. A new role or behavior can make a person feel "like an imposter," as Sheila puts it. Giving ourselves permission to make mistakes—to not know everything—is a first step in dealing with the fear of doing something new. Also helpful is seeking out mentors—peers, supervisors, or others whose skills we respect—to get constructive feedback about what we are doing.

We can also learn a lot from children's families. Sheila sought information and insights about Lilly from family members and found their input extremely valuable. Honoring families' knowledge about their own child is crucial to building partnerships. Listening to and taking seriously parents' perspectives even when they differ sharply from our own, we must also search for the shared goals that lie beneath our differences. When we find agreement with families on what we are working toward, we can use our shared goals to help us focus our energy.

In my dialogue with Sheila, I was struck by how hard most of us find it to open up difficult conversations with families or colleagues. Yet when we avoid these conversations, we usually make matters worse. Collaboration requires constant communication and negotiation. Identifying concerns is a positive step toward dealing with them. At the same time we must be sure to keep conversations focused on solving problems instead of blaming others or justifying ourselves.

**T**hink about how you give information to others when it is difficult or uncomfortable to do so. Do you plunge right in? Do you tend to soften the message so much that it isn't clear? What do you do to make it comfortable for both the listener and yourself?

**V**ideotape a conference or meeting you are having with a family or co-worker. As you watch the tape, observe how you are communicating, and how the other person or persons communicate with you. Are there any misunderstandings? What have you learned? (Be sure to explain to all involved how this tape will be used and who will see it. You will need everyone's written permission.)

**R**epresent your own balance scale, weighing the pros and cons of collaboration from your own perspective. Use words, symbols, or pictures on either side of the scale. In small groups discuss these issues.

O ur preschool has two classes of 3-year-olds and two of 4- and 5-year-olds with approximately 10 to 12 children in each class, along with a teacher and aide. The school is in a homey two-story house surrounded by maple and pine trees. We often see squirrels, chipmunks, rabbits, and birds in our playground. It is an ideal location for children to explore nature through walks around the neighborhood. Here are some of our thoughts.

**B:** My collaboration with Patty began three years ago when I was the lead teacher and Daniel, a child for whom she was the resource teacher, entered our program. Patty is an exceptional teacher, highly committed to her profession and her students. I enjoy her quirky sense of humor and admire the way she fights for the rights of each child with whom she works.

**P:** As a resource teacher I work with the child, his or her family, and the classroom teacher to implement an Individualized Education Program. Blanca is the kind of classroom teacher who gives children the opportunity to play and experiment in a warm and open environment. She is always willing to give children a chance. She seems to have a soft spot for a child when other teachers have declared, "I don't want that child in my classroom!" She is truly happy to see each and every child.

## Building trust

**B:** Daniel was 3 when he came into my classroom. Evaluations suggested that he was mildly mentally disabled, and I was told he was often aggressive.

**P:** Daniel's bad temper had made a strong impression during assessments. There were many concerns about what Daniel's behavior would be like in a preschool setting.

*Blanca Bandera, B.S., taught preschool for several years. Currently she teaches preschoolers with special needs for the South Bend Community School Corporation in Indiana.*

*Patty Burke, B.S., taught preschool for several years and is currently a preschool inclusion teacher for the South Bend Community School Corporation in Indiana.*

> *When a child repeatedly engages in undesired behaviors, Blanca and I try to figure out what the child is getting from the behavior. Why is he doing what he's doing?*

I knew from the very first time I met Blanca that her classroom could work for Daniel. She structured the environment so that Daniel could succeed and his behavior wouldn't drive the other children (and their parents) crazy. When a child repeatedly engages in undesired behavior, Blanca and I try to figure out what the child is getting from the behavior. Why is he doing what he's doing?

With Daniel, Blanca invested a lot of time and thought. She and I talked at length about how to make it work. When there was frustration, she did not lose her temper but used her words and actions to show Daniel that he was safe. She kept the environment consistent and helped him know that she still liked him even when she didn't like his actions.

**B:** When Daniel first enrolled in my classroom, there were many ups and downs. Some days Patty and I would think he had made tremendous progress, and then another day he would jump off tables and charge into other children. Initially Daniel showed a lot of anger and displayed aggressive behavior without any provocation.

His speech problems were very upsetting for him when he was unable to communicate to another child or a teacher. Once when Daniel had been having a particularly difficult day, it came to a head on the playground. He slapped another child because he wanted the swing she had. When I took him inside to calm him down, he became even more aggressive. He pulled my hair and tried to slap and kick me. As I held him, he constantly repeated, "I hate you."

About that time Patty walked in. She quickly came to me and asked how she could help. She did not try to take over the situation. She respected how I was dealing with Daniel and offered to help in any way she could. She asked if she should help the other teacher outside or help me hold and calm Daniel. I asked her to stay with me. Together we reasoned with Daniel and took turns reassuring him. After 10 minutes Daniel was ready to return to the playground under close supervision. One of many high points in my relationship with Patty, this incident confirmed my sense that I could count on her help and that she trusted my judgment.

**P:** Daniel is 5 now and still attends one of the preschool classes. The growth and change in his personality are miraculous. A very loving child, he gives lots of hugs and is a friend to all the children. He has learned to trust others and no longer exhibits aggressive behavior. Daniel is a success at school. Next year he will go to kindergarten, and I hope his teacher can continue to build on the foundation Blanca has given him.

**B:** I believe that Daniel's success now is largely due to the positive collaboration that Patty and I established. Many teachers would not have dealt with Daniel in their classrooms because his behavior was so disruptive. But because Patty gave me a lot of good ideas and strong moral support, I was able to respond positively to Daniel.

Patty is helpful and values every job in the preschool as important. When she comes, she doesn't just stand by, observe, and take notes. Patty is an active member of our preschool team. As soon as she enters the classroom, she jumps right in and helps in any way she can. If she is not playing with a child, she is cleaning tables, washing paint brushes, wiping up spills, helping set up the snack, and so on. Patty's willingness to help and become part of our classroom is one of the main reasons that our collaboration works.

**P:** One of the most important things I have learned in working with Blanca is the need for the classroom teacher to establish a primary bond with every child, including the child for whom I am the resource teacher. She is the one who will see this child every day. When I am in the classroom I do not focus all of my concentration on the child with special needs. I often work with the child within a small group of children.

**B:** It helps that Patty and I share a lot of the basic ideas about early childhood education. From the first time that Patty came to our preschool and we discussed how vital play is to a child's development, I knew I had a colleague.

**P:** I was so excited to think that someone else had ideas similar to mine about early childhood. Blanca and I have different backgrounds, but we share strong ideas about building trust in young children and helping them to be confident in playing independently. Our discipline styles are also similar.

## Developing communication

**B:** Of course good communication is vital to our collaboration. Patty updates me constantly about the status of the children we jointly support. She generally calls two to three times a week to inquire about a child and ask me to share information with her. She encourages me to call her if I have questions or concerns. Patty's continual efforts to share information enable me to deal effectively with Daniel and the other children with special needs who have been placed in my classes.

**P:** Blanca's teaching schedule typically prevents her attending the initial meeting held with each family to develop the child's Individualized Education Plan (IEP). I always go over with her the goals and objectives that have been identified in the plan, and we discuss when different therapists will come to the school to work with the child. I try to be at school on the first day of class so the children I'm placing will see a familiar face.

In November Blanca and I cooperate in doing parent-teacher conferences. We spend time before the meetings talking about the progress we see and what areas we each think needs more attention. The level of communication between Blanca and me, I believe, gives parents a sense of security; they know we are in sync as we plan for and work with their child. Together we answer each family's questions and ask for parents' insights to help resolve issues.

At the end of a school year, we have another conference with parents to write an IEP for the next year. By this time there is solid teamwork and a good exchange of ideas among all of us. Blanca makes parents feel welcome and important and addresses critical issues in a way that is not threatening or intimidating.

Seeing each child as an individual, Blanca is able to help all the children placed in her classroom have successful experiences. I am Blanca's partner and ally; I am not her supervisor, boss, or judge. Every time I visit her classroom, I learn something new.

**B:** Our collaboration is successful because Patty and I respect each other's opinions and contributions. Both of us are committed to meeting the needs of each child, and I think this is essential. Without our positive collaboration, I am convinced, the children in my classroom would have less success in the inclusive environment.

**P:** In working with community teachers, I try to be proactive —to anticipate problems and head them off. I get a sense of a teacher's strengths, likes, and dislikes, and I work to respect the rules, procedures, and schedule of the center and the classroom. My role is to support what is going on there.

Despite all this effort, do I encounter problems in collaboration? I do. Usually I begin to work out the problem by talking it over with my supervisor. A new perspective often helps me solve the problem.

Recognizing that I have a hard time working with highly structured academic sites that do not understand the developmental needs of children, I communicate with parents about good early childhood practices. Finding placements that will be a good fit for children and their families is key. Believing so strongly in the value of communication, I arrange my schedule to give me time to talk to

*Experiencing this communication breakdown in a collaboration in which I thought we were on the same wave length, I am more aware than ever of how communication can't be taken for granted.*

the community teachers. When we don't agree, having a chance to discuss differences helps to resolve conflict.

**B:** After having worked with two extremely talented special education teachers in successful collaborative efforts, I myself am now in the role of special educator. The challenges of collaboration from this side are different. Dealing with various personalities, teaching styles, and philosophies can be difficult, especially if I do not agree with the classroom teacher on important decisions affecting a child's educational program.

Here's an example I am still trying to puzzle through. In this case I had established a positive working relationship with the community teacher: we communicated extensively, evaluated Erica's progress, and discussed various ways to modify the environment to meet her special needs.

I was pleased to see Erica having such a successful experience, fitting in with the classroom, and having many positive peer interactions. I was very proud of this community placement. But in the spring when it was time to review and develop a new IEP for Erica, I had some surprises. At the IEP conference the classroom teacher expressed concerns she had not previously voiced. Focusing on the skills Erica had not yet accomplished and emphasizing her developmental delays, she argued that unless Erica moved to a self-contained classroom she would not do well. The parents and supervisor were confused: the teacher and I were expressing entirely opposite views about Erica's development and what should happen next.

The IEP committee decided to place Erica in a different community site in the fall. After the conference I found it somewhat awkward to work with the community teacher, but for the rest of the school year I tried to be positive and friendly. Experiencing this communication breakdown even in a collaboration in which I thought we were on the same wavelength, I am more aware than ever of how crucial communication is—and how it can't be taken for granted.

# Blanca's and Patty's mentor reflects . . .

In Blanca's and Patty's writing, I see the strengths they each bring to their work with young children. Any one with whom we collaborate contributes to the situation her or his own personality, skills and knowledge, communication style, and preferences, often different from our own. Recognizing the value of what the other person brings to the collaboration is important; effective collaborators build on each other's strengths and skills to meet the challenges before them.

In getting to know Blanca and Patty, I was struck by their flexibility. Rigid adherence to roles, I have noticed, undermines many collaborative efforts. Those who are involved in the lives of young children need to be especially flexible to meet the needs that emerge from moment to moment. As Blanca and Patty point out, a person's willingness to pitch in to get the job done goes a long way toward giving others the trust and comfort essential for a good collaborative relationship. Although discussions that clarify our expectations about roles can be helpful, role clarification is very different from seeing a task or need and thinking or communicating, "That's not my job!"

Trust builds over time, but at the beginning of collaborative relationships, finding opportunities to communicate respect for each other's skills is an important first step. We can also agree to ask each other for what we need to be successful in collaborating. Our needs will not always mesh, but the resulting conversation helps to create a climate of mutual respect.

Even when we know that communication is the key to successful collaboration, finding time to talk can be quite a challenge. Surrounded by young children, adults soon learn that finding time to talk together does not magically appear. We must value communication enough to set aside the time with our colleagues and with parents of the children in our care. Patty and Blanca have created time both for mini-talks during their classroom time together and for longer discussions outside the classroom.

**T**hink of a situation in which you did not communicate as effectively as you would have liked. What hampered this conversation or meeting? What did you learn from this experience?

**I**nterview someone you think is a good communicator. Ask about the techniques the person uses in giving information and listening.

**U**sing a metaphor (such as a baseball team playing a game), think about the people you work with. Who would each person be in this metaphor? While thinking about this metaphor, think about your own role (e.g., pitcher, catcher, coach?).

**I**ndividually create a Top 10 list of your own classroom beliefs. Then meet with team or center staff to compare and contrast your lists. Work together to create one list.

## Resources for further exploration of this topic

### Books and articles

Ayers, W. 1989. *The good preschool teacher*. New York: Teachers College Press.

Bruder, M.B. 1994. Working with members of other disciplines: Collaboration for success. In *Including children with special needs in early childhood programs*, eds. M. Wolery & J.S. Wilbers, 45-70. Washington, DC: NAEYC.

Chrislip, D.D., & C.E. Larson. 1994. *Collaborative leadership*. San Francisco: Jossey-Bass.

Friend, M., & L. Cook. 1995. *Interactions: Collaboration skills for school professionals*. 2d ed. White Plains, NY: Longman.

Klein, S., & S. Kontos. 1993. *Best practices in integration inservice training model: Guidebook*. Project final report, part 1. Bloomington: Indiana University.

Klein S., & S. Kontos. 1993. *Best practices in integration inservice training model: Instructional modules*. Project final report, part 2. Bloomington: Indiana University.

Pugach, M.C., & L.J. Johnson. 1995. *Collaborative practitioners, collaborative schools*. Denver: Love.

### Community contacts

Contact local public organizations serving children or adults and inquire about staff who are knowledgeable and/or do training for collaboration or networking.

# Epilogue

W e make no attempt here to sum up the many experiences, ideas, and feelings that these teachers have shared. Instead, we briefly outline aspects of the Best Practices in Integration—Outreach project that we see as key to its success. Three basic themes pervaded all aspects of the project—relationship-based training and support, reflection, and systems change—and their importance was confirmed in the changes the teachers made in understanding and practice, both during and after the project.

## Relationship-based training and support

Productive relationships foster change processes. To develop and maintain such relationships, we found, requires listening to teachers' voices, accepting their feelings, and both respecting and challenging their ideas. When conditions provide support for this quality of interaction, teachers are able to examine their assumptions and their practice, to experiment with and eventually consolidate change.

An environment in which participants feel free to discuss their doubts and mistakes also enables individuals to learn from one another. We continue to learn how to provide such conditions. A number of the specific techniques and approaches we have found useful are described in the Appendix. Our commitment to relationship-based work was reflected in both the training and mentoring components of the project.

**Training.** Wanting teachers to participate meaningfully in shaping the topics and issues addressed in training, we began by meeting with participants to find out what they were interested in and to learn about their classrooms and communities. Observing their classrooms directly further enabled us to anticipate what each teacher would bring to the training experience—the individual's range of experience, strengths, limitations, and resources. What we learned about participants and their programs allowed us to tailor the content and processes of training.

Real learning and change require active involvement. From the start of training we made explicit the expectations on both sides. Trainers established guidelines to create a safe climate in which all participants could express and explore their viewpoints. Working actively to encourage each individual's sense of strength, competence, and willingness to take risks, trainers provided structures for respectful disagreements and debate of controversial issues. Trainers conveyed information but kept their presentations brief to make time for more participatory activities. Participants had the opportunity to tell their stories, listen to others' stories and concerns, and share questions and reactions.

**Mentoring.** In addition to the training, the project provided mentoring and support that was designed to nurture collaborative problem solving and establish ongoing support mechanisms. Before and after each training session, mentors worked with individuals focusing on areas in which they wanted to examine and strengthen their practice. Between sessions participants wrote about or otherwise documented their experiences, growth, personal values, and philosophies. Mentors assisted the participants in maintaining their focus until some mastery had been achieved, only then moving on to another goal. More detail about these approaches is also provided in the Appendix.

## Reflection

Reflection was emphasized in all aspects of training and mentoring. We encouraged ongoing thinking about the training and its effects. Project participants encouraged each other to revisit familiar routines and formulas and engage in regular, collaborative, and reflective consideration of practices. They became comfortable with "doing, learning, and coming to know" (Tremmel 1993, 438).

Nurturing change in teachers' practices, especially related to collaboration, resulted in improved relationships with children and families and with the professionals who worked with them. Effects of this improvement, we hope, continue to ripple out and ultimately change systems.

## Change and changing systems

Learning is empowering when it is individually meaningful and self-directed. If we want education systems—schools and other early childhood settings, professional development institutions, and the like—to be learning organizations, the opportunities for developing communities of learners must expand. We must encourage new models of human service that foster problem solving through empowering interactions and collaborations.

Reflection at the individual and collective levels supports continuous improvement of practice. Educators and other professionals must engage in these processes regularly and actively. Being able to listen to and value others' perspectives and expertise does not always come easily to professionals trained to teach or "impart wisdom." In teacher education programs, learning to communicate effectively with other adults typically receives little attention. Trainers, adult educators, and supervisors must learn and practice the skills and techniques that nurture collaborative skills in practioners.

Our work suggests the fruitfulness of bringing together early childhood and special education professionals to listen to each other, discuss issues, and find common goals. Together these reflective practitioners can collaborate to create more effective, inclusive environments for all children and families.

### References and other resources

Clift, R., W.R. Houston, & M. Pugach. 1990. *Encouraging reflective practice in education.* New York: Teachers College Press.

Cohen, N.H. 1995. *Mentoring adult learners: A guide for educators and trainers.* Malabar, FL: Krieger.

Cowan, J. 1998. *On becoming an innovative university teacher.* Philadelphia: Society for Research into Higher Education and Open University Press.

Fenichel, E. 1992. Zero to Three Work Group on Supervision and Mentorship: Learning through supervision and mentorship to support the development of infants, toddlers, and their families. In *Learning through supervision and mentorship: A source book,* ed. E. Fenichel, 9-17. Arlington, VA: Zero to Three.

Gilkerson, L., & H. Als. 1995. Role of reflective process in the implementation of developmentally supportive care in the newborn intensive care nursery. *Infants & Young Children* 7 (4): 20-28.

Green, M. 1986. Reflection and passion in teaching. *Journal of Curriculum and Supervision* 2 (1): 68-87.

Parker, S. 1997. *Reflective teaching in the postmodern world.* Philadelphia: Open University Press.

Reiman, A.J., & L. Thies-Sprinthall. 1998. *Mentoring and supervision for teacher development.* New York: Longman.

Tremmel, R. 1993. Zen and the art of reflective practice in teacher education. *Harvard Educational Review* 63 (4): 434-58.

Vinz, R. 1996. *Composing a teaching life.* New York: Teachers College Press.

Witherall, C., & N. Noddings, eds. 1991. *Stories lives tell: Narrative and dialogue in education.* New York: Teachers College Press.

# **Appendix**

## *Reflective change techniques*

One should not train by formula any more than one should teach by formula. Yet hearing of others' experience may be valuable. For interested readers who are involved in teachers' professional development and change, we offer a brief summary of the key concepts and methods that evolved and proved effective in the Best Practices in Integration—Outreach project.

---

### Using Labels with Care

In all of our techniques for reflective change, using language responsibly when referring to children with special needs, as well as to children who are typically developing, is important. The value of using labels is in helping make sense out of the confusion of characteristics that can affect children and the adults who work with them. Being respectful of this function, it is also important to be aware of the dangers in using labels.

Children must be seen as individuals first, with their own uniqueness and potentials. Learning to speak of someone as a person first and as having a disability later is an important part of training. One can say, "Laura, who has autism," for example, rather than "the autistic child, Laura." Teachers show respect for each child as an individual in this way; they contribute to the sense of seeing all children as "ours"; and they model *respect* for other adults. In the Best Practices in Integration—Outreach project, training participants practiced the art of using labels sensitively and appropriately.

---

## 1. Setting the tone for training

Beginning the training with a clear statement of expectations helps to clarify each person's role and the ground rules that all agree to follow. For example, some standards include the following:

- Everyone is expected to participate.
- Each individual can exercise the right to pass.
- Accept no put-downs or disrespect.
- Listen carefully to others before responding.
- Use the five-minute rule (see details in technique # 6).
- Communicate your concerns about the experience.

When these rules are stated and accepted by all, participants feel a greater degree of psychological safety, which enables them to take risks. Comfort matters too. Room temperature and physical arrangement, scheduled breaks and self-care time, as well as a facilitator/trainer skilled at managing group process are important components of the training setting.

By acknowledging the skills and competencies each person brings to the project, trainers help participants feel confident and willing to take new risks. Using humor sets a positive tone for the training and puts participants at ease.

Making it possible for participants to build relationships between themselves and with the trainers in many different ways gives a structure that's conducive to exploration and growth. In our training we worked to create a climate that encourages controversy and constructive debate.

## 2. Scheduling individualized training

In the Best Practices project, training sessions were developed on the basis of each community's needs and timetable. Deemphasizing the "expert" role of the trainer meant spending less time in presenting information and more time in engaging the participants in their own learning. A typical half-day session followed a sequence like this.

*Introductions*—Who are we, what are our roles, and why are we here? Each person has the opportunity to speak personally to these questions.

*Establish group norms*—Emphasize safety and comfort, establish agreed-upon norms and rules, discuss risk taking and debate, and agree on how the group will conduct itself. For example, is raising hands expected?

*Ice-breaker activity*—Participants begin establishing relationships with others.

*Reflection activity*—Ask participants to think and talk about themselves in relation to specific topics and find a way to express their thoughts.

*Brief topical presentation* (approximately 30 minutes).

*Reinforcement/application activity*—Provide role-play or other activity-based means to use ideas expressed in the presentation.

*Application to personal work*—Ask participants to apply the topic at hand to their own classroom or to their professional skills and experiences in small groups, large groups, or individually, and to another topic or common concern.

A full-day session incorporates at least one more cycle of these activities.

### 3. Individualizing active learning

Informed by the Reggio Emilia approach and Howard Gardner's work on multiple intelligences, the Best Practices project designed training that offered a variety of ways to construct knowledge and challenge current practices. Encouraging participants to develop relationships within the group supports this goal. Maintaining a set of resources (including speakers, simulation games, role-play approaches, readings, visuals, video- and audiotapes, and jigsaw activities) is essential in providing individually appropriate ways to construct knowledge and extend or change current practices. Offering such resources during self-selected activity portions of the training allows individuals to learn in a variety of ways. Some participants may process information by thinking about it in the context of an event, a specific child, or a situation in their own classroom. Another way to extend thinking and learning is by reading novels and stories rather than expository texts, viewing movies rather than training tapes, and using other artistic forms rather than strictly empirical interpretations of ideas.

### 4. Listening to "no"

When presenters and trainers ask participants to consider new ideas, they must consider the natural resistance that comes from being asked to question and give up current practices, practices which have been adopted for specific reasons. As trainers in the Best Practices project, we used a variety of skills and sensitivities to increase our ability to understand and accept participants' lack of receptivity to recommended "best practices." Time and understanding, as it turned out, contributed more to the change process than new information or pressure. Skilled use of group and individual mentoring processes also contributed to an acceptance of participants' responses, "I can't" or "I won't," as but one step on their way to considering alternatives and ultimately changing.

### 5. Assessing the needs of adult learners

It is important to take the time to meet with teachers and administrators to find out their interests. In our training project, learning about the classrooms and communities began the process of connection and assured that the subsequent training would be relevant. Project staff observed participants' classrooms to understand what each group had to work with, the teachers' strengths and limitations, and the resources that were available. Listening to professionals talk about what they felt they *couldn't* change was also important.

A number of resources exist for assessing the learning needs of individuals who come to training. For example, the learning domains specified in the guidelines for professional preparation of special educators and early childhood educators can be adapted for purposes of self-assessment (NAEYC, DEC/CEC, & NBPTS 1996). Participants can rate their own levels of competency and prioritize their needs in the development of their learning contract.

### 6. Using the "five-minute rule"

This technique encourages perspective taking and openness to opposing viewpoints (Elbow 1986). Calling forth the rule, a group is asked first to take one side of a view on an issue (for example: "Gun play in classrooms is appropriate and should be allowed") and to see only the positive sides of that view for five minutes. Then the alternative approach ("Gun play is not appropriate and should not be allowed") is explored for five minutes.

The five-minute rule lets participants look at a controversial issue from two sides, reconsider their previous beliefs, and exercise tolerance for opposing points of view. In the Best Practices project, this technique was introduced at the beginning of group training and practiced on a neutral topic (such as,

"It's better to write with a pen than a pencil"). All participants were encouraged to invoke use of the rule as needed.

## 7. Creating ownership of learning

Shifting toward a co-constructed approach, the project trainers adopted techniques that encouraged participants to "own" their development and growth. Individual learning contracts spelled out what we would provide for the participants (workshops, mentoring, technical assistance) and what the participants would be responsible and accountable for. Here's one example of a participant learning contract (Hiemstra & Sisco 1990).

---

Learning contract for _____

                                   *(name of project, course, etc.)*

Participant's name _____ Date _____

What are you going to learn (objectives)?

How are you going to learn it (resources and strategies)?

Target date for completion.

How are you going to know that you have learned it?

How are you going to prove that you learned it (verification by others)?

---

## 8. Keeping the learning alive

Of course we want to encourage participants' reflection outside the training experience itself. Like Reggio Emilia classrooms, we also wanted to document and keep a history of learning for participants. To help them revisit their beliefs long after a session ends, a memory board was kept at each training session. Participants were asked to add an idea, thought, question, or concern on a sticky note, note card, or more elaborate document and to post it on the board before leaving. These memories were transcribed or otherwise recorded (sometimes photographed) and sent to everyone before the next session. Trainers began each new session by reviewing these memories to see what people had been working on and what progress or problems they were encountering with the new approaches they were trying.

Sometimes controversy provided an opportunity for homework. Participants were asked to come to their next session with a positive view of the topic under discussion or a reflection about how the topic affected their own practice.

### 9. Making change collaboratively

Training participants bring well-established sets of assumptions about themselves and their roles into the learning and change process. It may mean that some are heavily invested in being "the expert," while others have no "buy-in" and maintain passivity and detachment. Creating an environment in which it is assumed each participant can exercise expertise takes effort. Reducing the use of technical jargon is important in this process, as is taking time to explain terms that are essential. The training must model and practice collaborative learning processes that allow participants to release their assumptions about their roles and to experiment with new ideas and approaches.

The Best Practices project training created diverse groups, took time to explore each person's expertise, avoided pigeonholing adult roles, and clarified each person's assumptions and concerns. In addition, the training worked toward an ethic in which the children and families with whom each participant worked were seen as *ours* rather than *mine* or *yours*. Group topics addressed common concerns and practices that could be examined collaboratively. Thus specific skill areas, such as working with children who have autism, were explored through individual technical assistance.

### 10. Beginning a journal

Each project participant was asked to keep a journal on one important issue or topic. Once participants chose topics, they were given the choice of working with a mentor, a collegial group, or alone. Each participant decided what this reflective journaling would look like. Some chose writing, others created a reflection by using pictures and images, and some expressed themselves on audio- and/or videotape.

The project provided a set of questions to stimulate the initial exploration of issues and encourage participants' self-discovery along the way.

- Why did you select your topic? Describe it.
- What challenges have you encountered with respect to this issue?

- What challenges have you encountered with respect to this issue?
- What feelings do these challenges and this issue arouse in you?
- What assumptions are you discovering that you hold? How did you discover them?
- Have you considered or are you considering changing any of them?
- What interactions with people, materials, and other resources have contributed to your thinking/reflection process?
- What changes can you describe in your thinking and practice? Be as specific as possible.
- Have you become more reflective? If so, how has that come about? How can you enhance your reflectivity?
- What does it take or would it take for you to change? How far will you be able to go in the process before you feel you are giving up too much?
- How do you or did you determine what to do or how to concentrate on it so as to effect change?

## References and other resources

Council for Exceptional Children. 1996. *What every special educator must know.* Reston, VA: Author.

Elbow, P. 1986. *Embracing contraries: Explorations in learning and teaching.* New York: Oxford University Press.

Hiemstra, R., & B. Sisco. 1990. *Individualizing instruction: Making learning personal, empowering, and successful.* San Francisco: Jossey-Bass.

NAEYC, DEC/CEC (Division for Early Childhood of the Council for Exceptional Children), & NBPTS (National Board for Professional Teaching Standards). 1996. *Guidelines for preparation of early childhood professionals.* Washington, DC: NAEYC.

# Information about NAEYC

## NAEYC is . . .

an organization of more than 103,000 members founded in 1926 and committed to fostering the growth and development of children from birth through age 8. Membership is open to all who share a desire to serve and act on behalf of the needs and rights of young children.

## NAEYC provides . . .

educational services and resources to adults and programs working with and for children, including

• *Young Children,* the peer-reviewed journal for early childhood educators

• **Books, posters, brochures, and videos** to expand your knowledge and commitment to and support your work with young children and families, including topics on infants, curriculum, research, discipline, teacher education, and parent involvement

• An **Annual Conference** that brings people together from all over the United States and other countries to share their expertise and advocate on behalf of children and families

• **Week of the Young Child** celebrations sponsored by more than 400 NAEYC Affiliate Groups to call public attention to the critical significance of the child's early years

• **Insurance plans** for members and programs

• **Public affairs** information and access to information through NAEYC resources and communication systems for conducting knowledgeable advocacy efforts at all levels of government and through the media

• **A voluntary accreditation system** for high-quality programs for children through the National Academy of Early Childhood Programs

• **Resources and services** through the National Institute for Early Childhood Professional Development, working to improve the quality and consistency of early childhood preparation and professional development opportunities

• **Young Children International** to promote international communication and information exchanges

For information about membership, publications, or other NAEYC services, visit the **NAEYC Website** at **http://www.naeyc.org**

---

*National Association for the Education of Young Children*
*1509 16th Street, NW, Washington, DC 20036*
*800-424-2460 or 202-232-8777*